Language
Arts

Grade 5

FlashKids

ISBN: 978-1-4114-0413-7

Please submit all inquiries to FlashKids@bn.com

Manufactured in China

Lot #:
30 29
07/18

Flash Kids
A Division of Barnes & Noble
122 Fifth Avenue
New York, NY 10011

Dear Parent,

This book was developed to help your child improve the language skills he or she needs to succeed. The book emphasizes skills in the key areas of:

- grammar
- punctuation
- vocabulary
- writing
- research

The more than 100 lessons included in the book provide many opportunities for your child to practice and apply important language and writing skills. These skills will help your child improve his or her communication abilities, excel in all academic areas, and increase his or her scores on standardized tests.

About the Book

The book is divided into six units:

- Parts of Speech
- Sentences
- Mechanics
- Vocabulary and Usage
- Writing
- Research Skills

Your child can work through each unit of the book, or you can pinpoint areas for extra practice.

Lessons have specific instructions and examples and are designed for your child to complete independently. Grammar lessons range from using nouns and verbs to constructing better sentences. Writing exercises range from the business letter to the research report. With this practice, your child will gain extra confidence as he or she works on daily school lessons or standardized tests.

A thorough answer key is also provided so you may check the quality of answers.

A Step toward Success

Practice may not always make perfect, but it is certainly a step in the right direction. The activities in this book are an excellent way to ensure greater success for your child.

Table of Contents

Unit 3: Mechanics

Unit 4: Vocabulary and Usage

Unit 5: Writing

Unit 6: Research Skills

Nouns

> A **noun** is a word that names a person, a place, a thing, or an idea.
> Use exact nouns to make clear pictures.
> *Examples:*
> person = girl   place = park   thing = door   idea = freedom

DIRECTIONS > Read each sentence. Write the nouns. Write *person, place, thing,* or *idea* after each noun to tell what the noun names.

1. Our sense of smell is located in the nose.

_____

2. Most people like the smell of delicious food, mowed grass, and clean rain.

_____

3. People get a lot of enjoyment from these special odors.

_____

4. Rotten eggs produce an unpleasant odor.

_____

5. The sense of smell can protect a person from danger.

_____

DIRECTIONS > Rewrite each sentence. Replace the underlined nouns with more exact words.

6. José likes the smells of <u>meat</u> cooking and <u>dessert</u> baking.

_____

_____

7. José and Frank sat in the <u>room</u> waiting for their <u>meal</u>.

_____

_____

Common Nouns and Proper Nouns

A **common noun** names any person, place, or thing. It begins with a lowercase letter.

Examples:

writer   state   month

A **proper noun** names a particular person, place, or thing. Each important word of a proper noun begins with a capital letter.

Examples:

Fred Gipson   Hawaii   February

DIRECTIONS ➤ Read the sentences. Underline each common noun and circle each proper noun. Rewrite each sentence, replacing the common and proper nouns with different ones.

1. The young scientist was born in Maryland.

_____

2. Many friends helped Benjamin Banneker.

_____

3. People throughout the United States still recall his accomplishments.

_____

_____

4. Banneker helped design Washington, D.C.

_____

5. This man had an unusually good memory.

_____

6. The astronomer spent many nights watching the stars and planets.

_____

7. Now, scientists are exploring Mars, Jupiter, and other planets.

_____

_____

8. What would Banneker think of the changes in his country?

_____

Singular and Plural Nouns

A **singular noun** names one person, place, thing, or idea.
Examples:

| hog | blouse | fox | liberty |

A **plural noun** names more than one person, place, thing, or idea. Make most nouns plural by adding *s* or *es*.
Examples:

| hogs | blouses | foxes | liberties |

DIRECTIONS > Write each underlined noun. Then, write *singular* or *plural* to tell what kind of noun it is.

1. A <u>tornado</u> does not last as long as a <u>hurricane</u> does.

_____

2. A tornado usually lasts only <u>minutes</u>, or at the most a few <u>hours</u>.

_____

3. Its <u>winds</u> are much stronger than a hurricane's.

_____

4. The hot <u>air</u> from a large forest <u>fire</u> can cause a tornado.

_____

5. Certain weather <u>conditions</u> are warning <u>signs</u> for a tornado.

_____

DIRECTIONS > Rewrite each sentence. Change each underlined singular noun to a plural noun. Make any other changes that are necessary.

6. The <u>girl</u> ate her <u>lunch</u> on the school <u>bench</u>.

_____

7. The young <u>lady</u> looked at the dark <u>cloud</u> overhead.

_____

8. A strong <u>wind</u> picked up a <u>box</u> of books by the library <u>door</u>.

_____

_____

Special Plural Nouns

Some nouns change spelling in the plural form. Other nouns have the same spelling in the singular and plural form.
Examples:

Change Spelling	Same Singular and Plural
woman–women	salmon
child–children	elk
tooth–teeth	deer
goose–geese	trout
hoof–hooves	sheep

DIRECTIONS ▶ **Complete each sentence by writing the plural form of the noun in ( ).**

1. Lisa caught four special _____ in that stream.
(trout)

2. These _____ told Lisa a story.
(fish)

3. They said that they were really _____.
(hero)

4. Two of them were really _____.
(woman)

5. The other two were really _____.
(man)

6. They had chased out all the _____ from their village.
(mouse)

7. This went against the _____ of the other people in the village.
(belief)

8. The village people thought that mice protected them from _____.
(wolf)

9. For a while, there had been four _____ in a field.
(ox)

10. Then, they had been turned into _____ in a barnyard.
(calf)

11. All the _____ in the village made fun of them.
(child)

12. Finally, their _____ were turned into fins.
(foot)

13. If they could eat bread, their _____ would return to normal.
(life)

Singular Possessive Nouns

A **singular possessive noun** shows ownership by one person or thing.
Add an apostrophe (') and *s* to most singular nouns to show possession.
Examples:

Natoh's cat   the cat's whiskers

DIRECTIONS ▸ **Write each sentence. Change the underlined words to form a singular possessive noun.**

1. <u>The mother of my friend</u> had a baby yesterday.

_____

2. <u>The teeth of the baby</u> are not in yet.

_____

3. <u>The head of the child</u> is still soft.

_____

4. <u>The tie of the bib</u> is torn.

_____

5. <u>The sheets of the crib</u> are pink.

_____

6. <u>The smile of the uncle</u> is happy.

_____

7. <u>The gift of the grandmother</u> is a new blanket.

_____

8. <u>The pleasure of the father</u> is easy to see.

_____

9. <u>The eyes of the infant</u> are blue.

_____

10. <u>The life of my friend</u> will be different now.

_____

Plural Possessive Nouns

A **plural possessive noun** shows ownership by more than one person or thing.
To form the possessive of a plural noun ending in *s* or *es*, add only an apostrophe (').
To form the possessive of a plural noun that does not end in *s*, add an apostrophe and *s* ('*s*).
Examples:

> trucks' tires   foxes' lair   children's lunches

DIRECTIONS ▸ Write each sentence. Change the underlined words to form a plural possessive noun.

1. Imagine the <u>surprise of the children</u>!

   _____

2. They found the <u>baby of the robins</u> on the sidewalk.

   _____

3. They returned it to the <u>nest of the parents</u>.

   _____

4. They watched the <u>activities of the adult birds</u> for a while.

   _____

5. The <u>fear of the birds</u> was apparent.

   _____

6. The <u>odor of the humans</u> was on the baby bird.

   _____

7. The bird was now the <u>responsibility of the young people</u>.

   _____

8. The <u>job of the students</u> was to find a shoe box.

   _____

9. The <u>job of the parents</u> was to find some soft lining.

   _____

Pronouns

A **pronoun** is a word that takes the place of one or more nouns.
Use pronouns to avoid repeating words.
A **singular pronoun** replaces a singular noun. The words *I, me, you, he, she, him, her,* and *it* are singular pronouns. Always capitalize the pronoun *I*.
A **plural pronoun** replaces a plural noun. The words *we, you, they, us,* and *them* are plural pronouns.
Examples:

The woman thought that *she* should go to the store.
She takes the place of *the woman.*

The travelers searched for a place *they* could spend the night.
They takes the place of *the travelers.*

DIRECTIONS ▷ **Read each pair of sentences. Draw a line under the pronoun in the second sentence. Circle the word or words in the first sentence that the pronoun replaces.**

1. Explorers came to Australia.

They were amazed by the strange native animals and plants.

2. An animal the size of a greyhound lived there.

It could leap like a grasshopper.

3. These animals are now known as kangaroos.

Some of them can cover 27 feet in one jump.

4. Two interesting birds of Australia are emus and cassowaries.

They cannot fly.

5. The early explorers told about the platypus.

It is a mammal that lays eggs.

6. Scientists of the time did not believe the stories.

They thought the stories were lies.

7. The coolabah of Western Australia is an interesting tree.

It can survive frost as well as 120 degree heat.

8. The official flower of Western Australia is called the kangaroo paw.

It looks like a paw and is even furry to the touch.

Subject Pronouns

A **subject pronoun** takes the place of one or more nouns in the subject of a sentence. The words *I, you, he, she, it, we,* and *they* are subject pronouns.
Examples:

> *He* brought a rat to school.
> *We* do not like rats.
> *You* can pet the rat.

DIRECTIONS → Rewrite each sentence. Replace the underlined word or words with a subject pronoun.

1. <u>My brother and I</u> read about the Wrights last week.

_____

2. It was <u>my brother</u> who found the book.

_____

3. <u>Wilbur and Orville Wright</u> grew up in Dayton, Ohio.

_____

4. <u>Their father</u> was a bishop there.

_____

5. <u>Their older sister, Katharine,</u> helped care for them.

_____

6. <u>A toy bicycle</u> was a gift from their father.

_____

7. <u>Wilbur Wright</u> was four years older than Orville.

_____

8. On December 17, 1903, <u>the world's first airplane flight</u> took place.

_____

9. <u>The first flight</u> lasted 12 seconds.

_____

10. <u>The next three flights</u> were 13 seconds, 15 seconds, and 59 seconds.

_____

Object Pronouns

An **object pronoun** follows an action verb, such as *see* or *tell*, or a word such as *about, at, for, from, near, of, to,* or *with.*
The words *me, you, him, her, it, us,* and *them* are object pronouns.
Examples:
> Chen took *it* to school.
> Grandpa had a gift for *me.*
> My cousin saw *you.*

DIRECTIONS ▷ **Rewrite each sentence. Replace the underlined word or words with an object pronoun.**

1. Darkness covered <u>the pine woods, the swamp, and the game wardens</u>.

   _____

2. The game wardens noticed <u>the light</u>.

   _____

3. Then, the game wardens saw <u>the alligator poachers</u>.

   _____

4. Two men and a woman were searching <u>the lake</u> for alligators.

   _____

5. The game wardens pushed <u>their boat</u> out of the brush.

   _____

6. The wardens raced toward <u>the poachers</u>.

   _____

7. The powerful engine moved <u>the boat</u> quickly over the water.

   _____

8. The poachers quickly dumped <u>two alligators</u> back into the water.

   _____

9. The wardens searched the inside of <u>the poachers' boat</u>.

   _____

Subject or Object Pronoun?

Remember that pronouns can be subjects or objects in sentences.

○ ○○ ○○ ○○○ ○○○ ○○ ○○○ ○○○ ○○○ ○○○ ○○○ ○○○ ○○○ ○○ ○○○

DIRECTIONS → Choose the pronoun in ( ) that correctly completes each sentence. Write it on the line. Then, circle *subject pronoun* or *object pronoun*.

1. _____ has studied kung fu for years.
   (He, Him)

   subject pronoun   *object pronoun*

2. The history of the martial arts is interesting to _____.
   (he, him)

   subject pronoun   *object pronoun*

3. _____ know about many great warriors.
   (We, Us)

   subject pronoun   *object pronoun*

4. One of _____ was a 13-year-old girl named Shuen Guan.
   (they, them)

   subject pronoun   *object pronoun*

5. _____ lived during the Jinn Dynasty, over 1600 years ago.
   (She, Her)

   subject pronoun   *object pronoun*

6. Her people had a nickname for _____.
   (she, her)

   subject pronoun   *object pronoun*

7. _____ called her "Little Tigress."
   (They, Them)

   subject pronoun   *object pronoun*

8. When her town was attacked by bandits, no one would fight _____.
   (they, them)

   subject pronoun   *object pronoun*

9. _____ was the only one brave enough.
   (She, Her)

   subject pronoun   *object pronoun*

10. Shuen Guan fought her way through _____ and went for help.
    (they, them)

    subject pronoun   *object pronoun*

Reflexive Pronouns

A **reflexive pronoun** refers to the subject of a sentence. The words *myself, yourself, himself, herself,* and *itself* are singular reflexive pronouns. *Ourselves, yourselves,* and *themselves* are plural reflexive pronouns.

DIRECTIONS Choose the reflexive pronoun in ( ) that correctly completes each sentence. Write the pronoun on the line.

1. I will help _____ enjoy this vacation.
   (myself, ourselves)

2. Last year Jerry bought _____ a book about Australia.
   (himself, yourself)

3. The book concerned _____ with the history of the land.
   (itself, themselves)

4. Jerry's sister Joan made _____ read the book.
   (herself, ourselves)

5. "Jerry and Joan, teach _____ about Australia before our vacation,"
   (yourself, yourselves)
   their mother said.

6. "That way, we can all enjoy _____ more," she continued.
   (myself, ourselves)

7. "Joan, buy _____ a good pair
   (yourself, yourselves)
   of walking shoes before the trip," said her father.

DIRECTIONS Write a reflexive pronoun on each line to complete the sentence.

8. My sister and I will be treating _____ to a trip.

9. She still has to buy _____ a ticket.

10. I have bought _____ some new clothes for the trip.

11. Susan, our travel agent, taught _____ the travel business.

12. Her partner, Mark, talked _____ into learning it, too.

Possessive Pronouns

A **possessive pronoun** shows ownership. Some possessive pronouns come before a noun. Some stand alone. Some possessive pronouns are *my, your, his, her, its, our,* and *their.*
Examples:

Joe lost *his* glove.
He lost it in *your* barn.
The new car is *ours.*

DIRECTIONS > Underline the possessive pronoun in each sentence. Then, write *before a noun* or *stands alone* to tell the kind of possessive pronoun used.

1. The members of the Dallas club wanted to send their team to the Olympic trials.

   _____

2. Its membership included just one person. _____

3. Babe Didrikson was proud that the position would be hers. _____

4. Her teammates were proud of Didrikson, too. _____

5. They knew that, at the end of the trials, the championship would be theirs.

   _____

6. "All our fans will be supporting you," they told Didrikson. _____

DIRECTIONS > Write the pronoun in ( ) that correctly completes each sentence.

7. Didrikson's fans were always impressed by the range of _____
   (her, hers)
   athletic abilities.

8. Two gold medals were _____ at the end of the 1932 Olympic Games.
   (her, hers)

9. Many fans followed her varied career, and she appreciated all _____
   (their, theirs)
   attention.

10. Of all the sports in which she competed, _____ favorite is swimming.
    (your, yours)

Agreement of Pronouns

A pronoun is a word that takes the place of one or more nouns. Pronouns show number and gender. The number tells whether a pronoun is singular or plural. The gender tells whether the pronoun is masculine, feminine, or neutral. The **antecedent** of a pronoun is the noun or nouns to which the pronoun refers. A pronoun should agree with its antecedent in number and gender.

DIRECTIONS ▷ Write the pronoun that correctly completes the second sentence in each pair. Then, circle the pronoun's antecedent in the first sentence.

1. Mr. Les Harsten did an experiment with plants. _____ investigated with sound.

2. The man used two banana plants. He exposed _____ to the same amount of light.

3. Les also gave both plants the same amount of warmth and water. _____ did, however, change one thing.

4. One of the plants was exposed to a special sound for an hour a day. _____ was a high-pitched hum.

5. That plant grew faster. In fact, _____ was 70 percent taller than the other plant.

6. All sounds won't work this way. Some of _____ can harm plants.

7. A recording of Harsten's sound is being sold. _____ is used by some plant growers.

8. Classical music works just as well with plants. _____ seem to thrive on it.

9. Hard rock music, however, does not work. _____ can stunt their growth.

10. You may want to play music for your plants. _____ may like it.

Adjectives

An **adjective** is a word that describes a noun or pronoun. Adjectives can tell how many, what color, or what size or shape. They can also describe how something feels, sounds, tastes, or smells.

You usually separate two adjectives with a comma.

Use vivid adjectives to paint clear word pictures.

Examples:

Two eggs were in the nest.

The *blue* stone was in a *small* box.

The *fat* cat has *soft* fur.

ⓞ ⓞⓞ ⓞⓞ ⓞⓞⓞ ⓞ ⓞ ⓞ ⓞ ⓞⓞ ⓞ ⓞⓞ ⓞ ⓞⓞⓞ ⓞⓞⓞ ⓞⓞ ⓞⓞ ⓞⓞ ⓞ

> **DIRECTIONS** → **Write each adjective that describes the underlined nouns. Then, write *what kind* or *how many* to identify what the adjective tells about the noun.**

1. The azalea is a spectacular <u>plant</u>.

_____

2. It has superb, beautiful <u>flowers</u>.

_____

3. It will grow wherever winter <u>temperatures</u> are not too low.

_____

4. There are many different <u>types</u> of azaleas.

_____

5. You can find azaleas with red, pink, violet, or white <u>flowers</u>.

_____

6. Azaleas do best in spongy, acid <u>soil</u>.

_____

7. They should be fed three or four <u>times</u> between the end of the flowering <u>season</u> and September.

_____

_____

8. Bright, colorful <u>flowers</u> make the azalea a special <u>plant</u>.

_____

Proper Adjectives

A **proper adjective** is formed from a proper noun.
Capitalize each important word in a proper adjective.

DIRECTIONS Underline the proper adjective in each sentence.
On the line, write the proper noun from which
it is formed. Use a dictionary if you need help.

1. Our modern Olympics come from an ancient Greek tradition.

_____

2. The chariot races were often won by Spartan men.

_____

3. An Athenian racer won three times in a row, starting in 536 B.C.

_____

4. After 146 B.C., Roman athletes also competed in the games.

_____

5. The 1988 Olympics took place in the Korean city of Seoul.

_____

6. In 1976, a young Romanian girl, Nadia Comaneci, had seven perfect scores in gymnastics.

_____

DIRECTIONS Complete each sentence by writing a proper adjective on the line. Form
the proper adjective from the proper noun in ( ).

7. Gertrude Ederle was the first woman to swim the _____ Channel.
(England)

8. Sonja Henie was a famous _____ ice skater.
(Norway)

9. Barbara Ann Scott was a _____ ice skater.
(Canada)

10. Several _____ skaters have won awards in international competition.
(America)

Predicate Adjectives

An adjective is a word that describes a noun. A **predicate adjective** follows a linking verb such as *is, seems,* or *looks.* When an adjective follows a linking verb, it can describe the subject of the sentence.

In some sentences, different adjectives in different positions describe the same noun or pronoun.

Examples:

Sam is *young* and *bold.*
That snake looks *scary.*

DIRECTIONS > Circle the adjective following the linking verb in each sentence. Write the noun or pronoun the adjective describes.

1. These peanuts are crunchy. _____

2. They taste very salty. _____

3. The skin on the peanut is red. _____

4. Those pumpkin seeds look delicious. _____

5. Pumpkin seeds once seemed inedible. _____

6. They have grown popular lately. _____

7. Some quick snacks are healthful. _____

8. Green apples are sometimes sour. _____

9. This common fruit is crisp and juicy. _____

10. A crispy vegetable can be noisy if you eat it. _____

DIRECTIONS > Write two adjectives to complete each sentence.

11. Bananas are _____.

12. Pickles taste _____.

13. Candy canes usually look _____.

14. During the summer, watermelons become _____.

15. With enough rain, pole beans will grow _____.

Articles and Demonstrative Adjectives

The words *a, an,* and *the* are called **articles**. Use *a* before a word that begins with a consonant sound. Use *an* before a word that begins with a vowel sound. Use *the* before a word that begins with a consonant or a vowel.
This, that, these, and *those* are called **demonstrative adjectives**.
Examples:

> Have you ever seen *an* owl?
> *The* owl is *a* nocturnal animal.
> *That* owl scared *those* people.

DIRECTIONS Choose the adjective in ( ) that best completes each sentence. Write it on the line.

1. Many people have _____ strange idea about naturalists.
   (a, an)

2. _____ people regard naturalists as weird.
   (This, These)

3. They think naturalists wander around in forests, eating roots and berries along

   _____ way.
   (an, the)

4. Not all naturalists fit _____ description.
   (this, those)

5. You could be _____ naturalist yourself.
   (a, an)

6. You could learn _____ names of trees.
   (a, the)

7. You could also know when _____ chestnut is ready for roasting.
   (a, an)

8. You could tell whether _____ clay is better than that clay.
   (this, these)

9. You could learn all _____ things easily.
   (this, these)

10. You could become one of _____ weird naturalists, too!
    (that, those)

Adjectives That Compare

Add *er* to most short adjectives to compare two nouns or pronouns. Add *est* to most short adjectives to compare more than two nouns or pronouns. Change the *y* to *i* before adding *er* or *est* to adjectives that end in a consonant and *y*.
Use *more* with some adjectives to compare two nouns or pronouns. Use *most* with some adjectives to compare more than two nouns or pronouns.
Examples:

This building is *taller* than that one.
The whale is the *largest* of all animals.
Diving is *more interesting* to watch than golf.
It may be the *most difficult* of all sports.

DIRECTIONS ▷ **Write the correct form of the adjective in ( ) to complete each sentence.**

1. Our trip to New Mexico was even (wonderful) than I expected. _____

2. The mountains there are the (beautiful) I have ever seen. _____

3. We saw Wheeler Peak, the (high) point in the state. _____

4. We visited a mine shaft that was (deep) than a mile. _____

5. Mining is one of the (big) industries in New Mexico. _____

6. Santa Fe, the state capital, is not the (large) city in New Mexico. _____

7. It is not the (easy) city to reach by plane. _____

8. The (unusual) place we saw was Carlsbad Caverns. _____

9. We had never seen (strange) rocks than those. _____

10. My brother was (excited) about seeing some bats than I was. _____

11. To me, the (interesting) place of all was Santa Fe. _____

12. It is one of the (old) cities in North America. _____

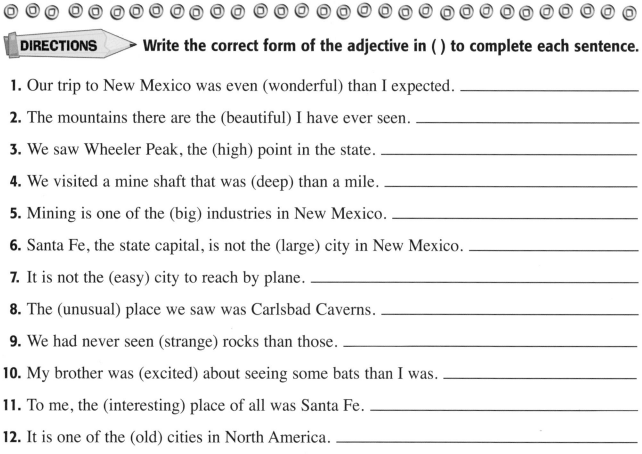

Special Forms of Adjectives That Compare

Some adjectives have special forms for comparing.
Examples:
> Trixi has a *good* story.
> Chad's story is *better* than Trixi's.
> Teena's story is the *best* of all.

Adjective	Comparing Two Things	Comparing More Than Two Things
good	better	best
bad	worse	worst
little	less	least
much	more	most
many	more	most

DIRECTIONS ▸ **Complete each sentence by choosing the correct form of the adjective in ( ). Write it on the line.**

1. Hunger brought the Irish to America for a _____ life.
   (better, best)

2. About half of Ireland's farms had _____ than three acres of land.
   (less, least)

3. They had had the _____ potato crop in years.
   (worse, worst)

4. Each day _____ people were starving than the day before.
   (many, more)

5. Queen Victoria was told that the situation was becoming _____ every day.
   (worse, worst)

6. She visited Ireland and said that she saw _____ ragged and wretched
   (more, most)
   people than she had seen anywhere else.

7. _____ Irish people chose Boston as their new home.
   (Many, Much)

8. Boston was the _____ convenient city for them because many ships
   (more, most)
   stopped there first.

Action Verbs and Linking Verbs

A **verb** expresses action or being.

An **action verb** is a word or group of words that expresses an action. An action verb is often the key word in the predicate. It tells what the subject does.

A **linking verb** connects the subject of a sentence with a word or words in the predicate. The most common linking verb is *be*. Some forms of *be* are *am, is, are, was,* and *were*. Here are other common linking verbs: *become, feel, seem, look, grow, taste, appear,* and *smell*.

Examples:

King Uther *ruled* England a long time ago. (action)

The name of his baby boy *was* Arthur. (linking)

In time, Sir Ector *became* Arthur's guardian. (linking)

DIRECTIONS Read each sentence. Underline each action verb. Circle each linking verb.

1. Young Arthur felt very nervous.

2. Sir Kay left his sword at the inn.

3. He needed his sword for the tournament that day.

4. Arthur looked all over the village for a replacement.

5. Suddenly, Arthur saw a sword in a stone.

6. He ran over to the stone and studied the strange sword.

7. It appeared very secure in its stony sheath.

8. Arthur pulled it, and it moved.

9. The sword slid from the stone easily!

10. Arthur hurried back to the tournament with his prize.

11. Sir Ector bowed deeply to his foster son.

12. The sword was the sign of the next king of England.

Main Verbs and Helping Verbs

Sometimes a simple predicate is made up of two or more verbs. The **main verb** is the most important verb in the predicate. It comes last in a group of verbs.
A **helping verb** can work with the main verb to tell about an action. The helping verb always comes before the main verb. These words are often used as helping verbs: *am, is, are, was, were, has, have, had,* and *will.*
Sometimes another word comes between a main verb and a helping verb.

DIRECTIONS ▶ **Choose the correct form of the verb in ( ) to complete each sentence. Write the word in the sentence. Then, write *main verb* or *helping verb*.**

1. Inez has _____ Greek legends to children for many years.
   (tell, told, telling)

_____

2. The children were _____ forward to the next story.
   (look, looked, looking)

_____

3. "I shall _____ the children the legend of Narcissus," she thought.
   (tell, told, telling)

_____

4. Narcissus _____ hunting one day.
   (shall, have, was)

_____

5. He had _____ over a mountain pool for a drink.
   (lean, leaned, leaning)

_____

6. He _____ gazing at his own reflection in the water.
   (are, was, were)

_____

7. Narcissus had _____ in love with his own face.
   (fall, fallen, falling)

_____

8. The next moment, a flower_____ growing where
   (am, are, was)
   Narcissus had stood.

_____

Present-Tense Verbs

A **present-tense verb** tells about actions that are happening now.
Add *s* or *es* to most present-tense verbs when the subject of the sentence is *he, she, it,* or a singular noun.
Do not add *s* or *es* to a present-tense verb when the subject is *I, you, we, they,* or a plural noun.
Examples:
Dougal Dixon *writes* books that stretch the reader's imagination.
His ideas *mix* science and fiction in an exciting way.
The neck of the lank *reach*es high into the air like a giraffe's.
The harridan *flies* with wings that fold up when it walks.

> **DIRECTIONS** Write the present-tense form of the verb in ( ) that correctly completes each sentence.

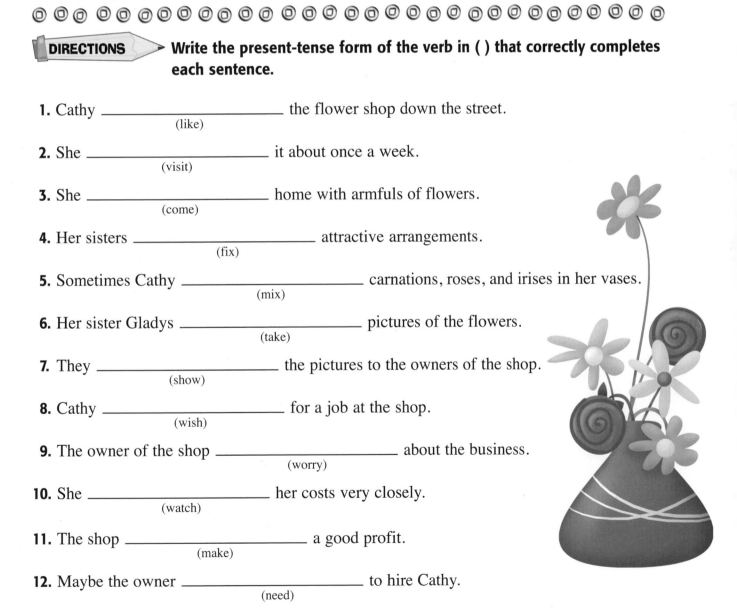

1. Cathy _____ the flower shop down the street.
(like)

2. She _____ it about once a week.
(visit)

3. She _____ home with armfuls of flowers.
(come)

4. Her sisters _____ attractive arrangements.
(fix)

5. Sometimes Cathy _____ carnations, roses, and irises in her vases.
(mix)

6. Her sister Gladys _____ pictures of the flowers.
(take)

7. They _____ the pictures to the owners of the shop.
(show)

8. Cathy _____ for a job at the shop.
(wish)

9. The owner of the shop _____ about the business.
(worry)

10. She _____ her costs very closely.
(watch)

11. The shop _____ a good profit.
(make)

12. Maybe the owner _____ to hire Cathy.
(need)

Past-Tense Verbs

A **past-tense verb** tells about actions that happened in the past.
Add *ed* or *d* to most present-tense verbs to make them show past tense. You may have to drop an *e*, double a final consonant, or change a *y* to an *i*.
Examples:

When Mr. King was a boy, he *lived* on a farm.
He always *carried* his lunch to school.
He *dipped* water from a nearby spring.

DIRECTIONS ▶ **Write the past-tense form of each verb in ( ) to complete each sentence.**

1. We _____ to the food fair.
(walk)

2. I _____ many different foods.
(sample)

3. Indian curry _____ both spicy
(seem)
and sweet.

4. Colorful signs _____ the unusual treats.
(describe)

5. A Greek restaurant _____ baklava made
(serve)
from nuts, honey, and flaky pastry.

6. My friend _____ a glass of African root beer.
(sip)

7. A woman _____ spring rolls made of shrimp and vegetables.
(fry)

8. I _____ many tasty foods that day.
(try)

9. One chef _____ me a red carnation.
(pass)

10. I _____ the flower onto my shirt.
(pin)

11. All of the meals _____ fresh vegetables and fruit.
(feature)

12. We _____ many unusual ones.
(taste)

Future-Tense Verbs

A **future-tense verb** expresses action that will happen in the future.
To form the future tense of a verb, use the helping verb *will* with the main verb.
Examples:
> Sam *will live* in the woods all year.
> He *will learn* about many things.

Sometimes other words appear between the helping verb and the main verb.
Examples:
> Sam *will* not *go* back to his home.
> *Will* he *have* a hard time in the winter?

DIRECTIONS ➤ **Complete each sentence. Write the future tense of the verb in ( ).**

1. What _____ _____ to Sam in the next few months?
(happen)

2. He _____ _____ for game.
(hunt)

3. He _____ _____ food at harvest time.
(gather)

4. _____ Sam _____ his family?
(miss)

5. _____ they _____ for him in the woods?
(search)

6. They probably _____ not _____ him.
(find)

7. Sam _____ _____ David, his friend.
(remember)

8. Perhaps Sam _____ _____ something different.
(cook)

9. Maybe Sam _____ _____ down the river on his new raft.
(float)

10. No matter what, Sam _____ _____.
(hide)

11. No one _____ _____ him.
(notice)

12. _____ Sam _____ the woods?
(leave)

Which Tense Is It?

Remember that a present-tense verb tells about actions that are happening now. A past-tense verb tells about actions that happened in the past. A future-tense verb shows action that will happen in the future.

DIRECTIONS ▷ **Underline the verb in each sentence. Then write _present, past,_ or _future_ to identify the tense.**

1. Lizards look different from snakes. _____

2. For one thing, they have legs. _____

3. A gecko lizard climbs across a ceiling. _____

4. Suction cups on its feet make this possible. _____

5. That lizard climbed the hill. _____

6. That other lizard jumps very high. _____

7. Samuel will see many lizards at the zoo. _____

8. He will go to the zoo on Tuesday. _____

9. We will ride to the zoo on a bus. _____

10. The zoo guide will tell us all about lizards. _____

DIRECTIONS ▷ **Change each present-tense verb to the correct future-tense form. Rewrite the sentence on the line.**

11. Sam sees ten lizards.

_____

12. I see only four.

_____

13. Some lizards change colors.

_____

Irregular Verbs

An **irregular verb** is a verb that does not end with *ed* to show past tense. Some irregular verbs show past tense by using a different form of the main verb with *have, has,* or *had.*

Examples:

Present	Past	Past with Helping Verb
do, does	did	(have, has, had) done
come, comes	came	(have, has, had) come
run, runs	ran	(have, has, had) run
go, goes	went	(have, has, had) gone

DIRECTIONS ▷ **Write the past-tense form of the verb in ( ) that correctly completes each sentence.**

1. Allison has _____ a report on chameleons.
(do)

2. She _____ a bus to the zoo to do research.
(ride)

3. She _____ some change to the bus driver.
(give)

4. At the zoo, Allison _____ from the entrance to the lizard area.
(run)

5. The chameleons had _____ out into the sunlight.
(come)

6. She _____ her lunch and watched the lizards.
(eat)

7. She _____ several chameleons, each a different color.
(see)

8. The guide had _____ hello to her.
(say)

9. Allison _____ twelve photos of the reptiles for her report.
(take)

10. She had _____ about her report for weeks.
(think)

11. She had _____ a rough draft already.
(write)

12. That afternoon, she _____ home and worked on the report.
(go)

Direct Objects

A **direct object** is a noun or pronoun that receives the action of the verb.
Use object pronouns such as *me, you, him, her, it, us,* and *them* as direct objects.
Examples:

The country of France gave the *Statue of Liberty* to the United States.
The French government shipped *her* in pieces to the United States.

DIRECTIONS ▷ **Read each sentence. Underline the direct object.**

1. A team of engineers and laborers constructed her.

2. The Statue of Liberty greeted many immigrants.

3. She carries a torch in her upraised hand.

4. To immigrants, she represents hope and freedom.

5. Ships full of immigrants passed the statue before arriving in America.

DIRECTIONS ▷ **Think of a direct object to complete each sentence. Write it in the blank.**

6. Millions of immigrants gave up _____ to come to America.

7. Immigrants sought _____ in America.

8. They first visited _____.

9. The immigration agents at Ellis Island questioned the _____.

10. The immigration agents processed _____ slowly.

11. Many immigrants could not speak _____.

12. Starting over in a new country required _____.

13. They faced many _____.

14. Immigrants found _____ in big cities.

15. Big cities also offered _____.

16. Immigrants who spoke the same language established _____.

Adverbs

An **adverb** is a word that describes a verb.
An adverb may tell how, when, or where an action happens. Many adverbs that tell how end in *ly*.
Use adverbs to make your writing vivid. Vary your sentences by moving the adverbs.
Examples:

> Kristen visited the Science Museum *yesterday*.
> She saw an exhibit of holograms *upstairs*.
> She *finally* learned why holograms look so real.

DIRECTIONS ▷ Circle the adverb that describes the underlined verb. Then, circle *where, when,* or *how* to indicate what the adverb tells.

1. Daedalus carefully <u>built</u> two pairs of wings.   *where   when   how*

2. First, he <u>collected</u> the feathers of birds.   *where   when   how*

3. Next, he <u>constructed</u> frames of wax.   *where   when   how*

4. Then, he <u>attached</u> the feathers to the frames.   *where   when   how*

5. Finally, he <u>put</u> the wings on himself and on his son, Icarus.   *where   when   how*

6. Daedalus firmly <u>warned</u> Icarus about the Sun.   *where   when   how*

7. The warmth of the Sun would surely <u>melt</u> the wax.   *where   when   how*

8. The father and son <u>flew</u> joyfully in the sky.   *where   when   how*

9. Icarus <u>flew</u> higher.   *where   when   how*

10. Soon, the Sun <u>melted</u> all the wax.   *where   when   how*

11. Icarus <u>fell</u> down into the sea.   *where   when   how*

DIRECTIONS ▷ Add an adverb to make each sentence more vivid. Write the new sentence.

12. Daedalus looked at the surface of the sea.

_____

13. Feathers drifted on the waves.

_____

Adverbs That Compare

Adverbs can be used to compare two or more actions.
When you compare two actions, add *er* to most short adverbs. When you compare more than two actions, add *est* to most short adverbs.
Use *more* and *most* before most adverbs that have two or more syllables. When you compare two actions, use *more*. When you compare more than two, use *most*.
The adverbs *well* and *badly* have special forms of comparison: *well, better, best; badly, worse, worst.*
Examples:
> Autumn comes *sooner* in Maine than in Virginia.
> You must drive *more carefully* in wet weather than in dry weather.
> This snowblower works *better* with dry snow than with wet snow.

DIRECTIONS ▷ **Write the correct form of the adverb in ( ) to complete each sentence.**

1. On August 3, 1492, the sailors aboard three small ships waited _____
(eagerly)

than they ever had.

2. Their captain had argued _____ than anyone else that the world was
(strongly)

round.

3. Of all the rulers at that time, Queen Isabella of Portugal acted _____.
(courageously)

4. She believed, _____ than King Ferdinand did, that this was a good idea.
(completely)

5. Columbus appealed to the queen _____ than another explorer did.
(often)

6. Of all the explorers at court, Columbus had stated his case _____.
(convincingly)

DIRECTIONS ▷ **Complete each sentence with the correct form of *well* or *badly*.**

7. Columbus did _____ than he ever thought possible.
(well)

8. At times, his crew thought they were doing _____ than any other
(badly)

crew in the history of the world.

9. Columbus had prepared _____ for this trip than for any other trip.
(well)

10. The three ships were equipped _____ for the journey.
(well)

Adverbs Before Adjectives and Other Adverbs

An adverb can be used to describe a verb. An adverb can also be used to describe an adjective or another adverb.
Example:
    Sheri did a *fairly good* job.
    She thought *very long* about the question.

DIRECTIONS ▷ Circle the adverb that describes the underlined adjective or adverb.

1. Reiko was sitting very <u>quietly</u> at her desk.

2. She felt extremely <u>interested</u> in the book.

3. The book was about carefully <u>planned</u> Japanese gardens.

4. Reiko quite <u>suddenly</u> decided to make one.

5. She knew her garden couldn't be too <u>big</u>.

6. She had a fairly <u>small</u> yard.

7. It was certainly <u>difficult</u> to choose a type of garden.

8. She considered the rather <u>complicated</u> job of making a garden with a pond.

9. Her yard was much <u>too</u> small for that.

DIRECTIONS ▷ Draw an arrow from the underlined adverb to the adjective, other adverb, or verb it describes.

10. A teahouse garden is <u>particularly</u> charming.

11. It <u>gently</u> suggests an approach to a mountain temple.

12. The builder <u>skillfully</u> uses rocks and stones to suggest mountains and valleys.

13. Reiko didn't think this would work <u>effectively</u> in her yard.

14. She <u>finally</u> decided on a dry landscape garden.

15. A dry landscape garden is <u>much</u> less expensive than a teahouse garden to create.

Adverb or Adjective?

Use an adverb to describe a verb. Use an adjective to describe a noun or pronoun. Use *good* as an adjective. Use *well* as an adverb or as an adjective to mean "healthy."

DIRECTIONS ▷ **Complete each sentence by writing the correct word in ( ).**

1. Have you ever brushed up _____ against a stinging nettle?
(gentle, gently)

2. Were you surprised by the _____ number of stinging sensations?
(great, greatly)

3. When this happens to you, you might _____ lift up a leaf.
(careful, carefully)

4. Notice that the underside is _____ covered with sharp bristles.
(complete, completely)

5. These are _____ attached to sacs of formic acid, the same acid you
(firm, firmly)
get from an ant sting.

6. Nettle stings are not _____ .
(serious, seriously)

7. The pain will go away _____ quickly.
(fair, fairly)

8. You can dab the _____ area with
(entire, entirely)
rubbing alcohol to soothe the pain.

DIRECTIONS ▷ **Complete each sentence with *good* or *well*.**

9. Tina and Ted went for a _____, long walk in the woods.

10. Tina had not been feeling _____ for a few days.

11. Tina and Ted both walk _____ .

12. They had packed a _____ lunch of sandwiches and apples.

Prepositions

A **preposition** is a word that relates a noun or pronoun to other words in the sentence. The **object of the preposition** is the noun or pronoun that follows the preposition. Some commonly used prepositions are in the box below.
Example:

>I went *to* the store.

A prepositional phrase is a group of words made up of a preposition, its object, and all the words that come between them. Prepositional phrases often tell where, what kind, when, or how.
Example:

>*At night* she guided her canoe *through the waves*.

above	below	from	through	after	between	into	around
by	of	under	at	during	off	until	before
except	on	up	behind	for	over	without	

DIRECTIONS ▸ **Read each sentence. Underline each prepositional phrase. Circle the object of the preposition.**

1. The girl returned to her island.

2. A leaking boat had nearly taken her below the waves.

3. She had traveled without any means of navigation except the stars.

4. For many centuries, sailors have found their position by the stars.

5. New developments in the 1700s made navigation easier.

6. However, even modern travelers on the sea use the ancient method of celestial navigation.

7. Navigators take the bearing of a star.

8. A sextant measures a star's angle above the horizon.

9. Sailors can tell their position from that reading.

10. Without this information, navigation would be a hard task.

Prepositional Phrases

Remember that a prepositional phrase is made up of a preposition, the object of the preposition, and all the words in between.

DIRECTIONS ▷ **Underline each prepositional phrase. Circle the preposition.**

1. Did you ever feel seasick in a car?

2. When you are seasick, you are not really sick from the sea.

3. You are sick from the motion of the waves.

4. In this same way, you can get sick in the back of a car.

5. Your sense of balance has been upset.

6. Deep inside your ears are semicircular canals.

7. These canals are filled with a fluid and are lined with special hairs.

8. These hairs pick up the sense of movement when you change position.

9. Usually, the fluid lies still in the bottom of the canals.

10. Quick, violent motions make the fluid move around the canals.

11. This can cause a sick feeling in your stomach.

DIRECTIONS ▷ **Add a prepositional phrase to each sentence. Write the new sentence on the line.**

12. Lying down may help you feel better.

_____

13. There is less motion in the front seat, so you might move.

_____

_____

14. Reading can make motion sickness worse, so don't ever read.

_____

_____

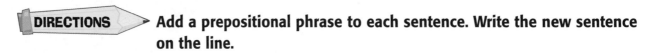

Preposition or Adverb?

Some words can be used as prepositions or adverbs.
Examples:
    The cat climbed *up* the tree.   We looked *up*.

DIRECTIONS ▸ Circle *preposition* or *adverb* to identify the underlined word in each sentence.

1. The Morgans were driving <u>down</u> the highway.

    preposition   *adverb*

2. Suddenly, the youngest child cried <u>out</u>.

    preposition   *adverb*

3. "Don't drive <u>through</u> the lake, Mom!" he shouted.

    preposition   *adverb*

4. The family looked <u>around</u>.

    preposition   *adverb*

5. <u>On</u> the road they saw shimmering patches of water.

    preposition   *adverb*

6. "It's just a mirage, David," his sister Camille said, looking <u>outside</u>.

    preposition   *adverb*

7. "No matter how far we drive, we will never even get <u>near</u> it," Camille explained.

    preposition   *adverb*

8. "On a day like this, a hot layer of air is <u>above</u> the road," said David's mother.

    preposition   *adverb*

9. "The hot layer of air is bending the light, as if <u>through</u> a prism," continued Camille.

    preposition   *adverb*

DIRECTIONS ▸ Add a prepositional phrase to each sentence.

10. The family continued to drive _____.

11. _____ they decided to stop.

12. They got out _____.

13. They looked _____.

Conjunctions

A **conjunction** is a word that joins words or groups of words.
Conjunctions may be used in several ways. The conjunction *and* is used to mean
"together." The conjunction *but* is used to show contrast. The conjunction *or* is
used to show choice.

Examples:

Patrick *and* the twins looked at their new home.
His mother felt sad, *but* Patrick was excited.
Might this old house hold mysteries *or* treasures?

DIRECTIONS Complete each sentence, using the conjunction that
has the meaning in ( ).

1. The house looked bare _____ gloomy.
   (together)

2. The twins began to cry, _____ Patrick cheered them up.
   (contrast)

3. Patrick walked from room to room _____ looked for trapdoors.
   (together)

4. He did not find any trapdoors _____ mysterious stairways.
   (choice)

5. Patrick was disappointed, _____ his parents were glad.
   (contrast)

6. They did not want a house with ghosts _____ goblins in it.
   (choice)

7. Patrick told them there might be treasure _____ gold instead.
   (together)

8. His mother _____ father thought he was being silly.
   (together)

9. The treasure could be in the cellar _____ in the backyard.
   (choice)

10. He found a coin in the backyard near the cellar door, _____ he knew
    (together)
    that he was right.

11. People were coming to work on the house, _____ Patrick was afraid
    (together)
    they would find the treasure first.

12. His parents might think it was silly, _____ Patrick would not stop
    (contrast)
    searching.

Interjections

An **interjection** is a word or a group of words that expresses strong feeling.
Examples:
> *Help*! I hurt my foot!
> *Wow*! How did you do that?

DIRECTIONS Circle the interjection in each item.

1. Gee! The baby is so tiny.

2. Wow! Her hands are so dainty.

3. She seems to be unhappy. Oh, dear!

4. Oh, my! What can we do to make her stop crying?

5. Good grief! That doesn't work.

6. Dad, where are you? Oops!

7. Great! Here comes Dad.

8. Alas! We cannot calm the baby. Can you help, Dad?

9. Of course! I'll show you what to do.

DIRECTIONS Add an interjection to each exercise to express strong feeling. Punctuate correctly.

10. _____ She smiled at me!

11. _____ I knew she recognized me. I'm her brother, after all.

12. _____ I think the baby is going to sneeze.

13. She already did. _____

14. _____ I just dropped the rattle.

15. _____ I hope she doesn't start crying again.

16. _____ I can't stand all this noise!

17. _____ When will we get some peace and quiet around here?

18. That will happen after she leaves for college. _____

What Is a Sentence?

A **sentence** is a group of words that expresses a complete thought. It always begins with a capital letter. It always ends with a punctuation mark.
Every sentence has two parts. The **subject** is the part about which something is being said. The **predicate** tells about the subject.

Subject   **Predicate**
My fifth-grade class   is going on a field trip.

The **complete subject** is all the words that make up the subject. A **simple subject** is the key word or words in the subject of a sentence. The simple subject tells whom or what the sentence is about.
The **complete predicate** is a word or group of words that tells something about the subject. The **simple predicate** is the key word or words in the complete predicate. The simple predicate is an action verb or a linking verb, together with any helping verbs.
Examples:

A long, yellow school bus is taking us to New York. (complete subject)
A long, yellow school bus is taking us to New York. (simple subject)
Our teacher sat up front. (complete predicate)
Our teacher sat up front. (simple predicate)

DIRECTIONS ➤ **Add a complete subject or a complete predicate to each sentence.**

1. Mr. and Mrs. Brown _____.

2. _____ got off the bus in New York.

3. Tall buildings _____.

4. Some students _____.

5. The field trip _____.

6. _____ wants to go again soon.

7. Next time, the adults _____.

8. Before the second trip, they _____.

9. _____ will make the trip a success.

Is It a Sentence?

Remember that a sentence is a group of words that expresses a complete thought. It always begins with a capital letter. It always ends with a punctuation mark.
Example:
> The capital of Illinois is Springfield.

⊚⊚⊚⊚⊚⊚⊚⊚⊚⊚⊚⊚⊚⊚⊚⊚⊚⊚⊚⊚⊚⊚⊚⊚⊚⊚⊚⊚⊚

DIRECTIONS ➤ **If the group of words is a sentence, write it correctly. Capitalize the first word, and end the sentence with a period. If the group is not a sentence, write *not a sentence*.**

1. we memorized the capitals of all of the states

_____

2. everyone knew the capital of Arkansas

_____

3. the capital is not always the largest city in the state

_____

4. you should picture the map in your mind

_____

5. the left side is the west side

_____

6. right through the middle of the country

_____

7. that river empties into the Gulf of Mexico

_____

8. the Hudson River valley in New York

_____

9. three people found Delaware right away

_____

10. a map of the thirteen original colonies

_____

Subjects and Predicates

Be sure your sentences have two parts, a **subject** and a **predicate**. The subject is the part about which something is being said. The predicate tells about the subject.

Subject
My whole family

Predicate
went to the mall.

DIRECTIONS Which sentence part is missing? Write *subject* or *predicate* on the line.

1. Your eyes _____.

2. Your other sense organs _____.

3. _____ pick up sounds.

4. _____ feel hot and cold.

5. The tongue _____.

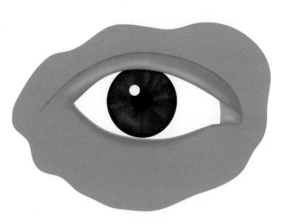

DIRECTIONS Read each sentence. Underline the subject. Circle the predicate.

6. The eye is made of many parts.

7. The pupil is the round, black center of the eye.

8. The outer, colored part is called the iris.

9. The iris is made of a ring of muscle.

10. Too much light can damage the eye.

11. The iris closes up in bright light.

12. Some people are colorblind.

13. They cannot see shades of red and green.

14. A nearsighted person cannot see distant things well.

15. Close objects are blurry to a farsighted person.

16. People who need glasses to read are farsighted.

Simple Subjects and Complete Subjects

Remember that the simple subject is the main word or words in the complete subject of a sentence. The complete subject includes all the words that tell whom or what the sentence is about.

Examples:

The county's <u>fair</u> was the best ever this year. (simple subject)

<u>The games on the midway</u> had good prizes. (complete subject)

DIRECTIONS ▸ **Read each sentence. Underline the complete subject. Then, write the simple subject on the line.**

1. Two young men were on their way from Dallas to Waco, Texas. ⎯⎯⎯⎯⎯⎯

2. A raging tornado was also on its way to Waco. ⎯⎯⎯⎯⎯⎯

3. Two square miles of the city would soon be twisted and destroyed. ⎯⎯⎯⎯⎯⎯

4. An odd roaring noise began with the rain. ⎯⎯⎯⎯⎯⎯

5. The strong wind tore buildings apart. ⎯⎯⎯⎯⎯⎯

6. Giant walls fell into the street. ⎯⎯⎯⎯⎯⎯

7. One side of a street was destroyed in Waco. ⎯⎯⎯⎯⎯⎯

8. The other side had not been touched. ⎯⎯⎯⎯⎯⎯

9. Some people were picked up by the wind. ⎯⎯⎯⎯⎯⎯

10. A tornado will sometimes set a person down gently. ⎯⎯⎯⎯⎯⎯

11. This lucky person may even be unhurt. ⎯⎯⎯⎯⎯⎯

12. Unlucky people may be set down violently by a tornado. ⎯⎯⎯⎯⎯⎯

13. Dorothy was among the lucky ones. ⎯⎯⎯⎯⎯⎯

14. She was set down safely in Oz. ⎯⎯⎯⎯⎯⎯

15. A ride in a tornado would be quite an experience. ⎯⎯⎯⎯⎯⎯

Compound Subjects

A **compound subject** is two or more simple subjects that have the same predicate. Join the two or more simple subjects in a compound subject with *and* or *or*.
Examples:

Sun *and* sand make Hawaii a popular vacation spot.
Surfing *or* swimming can be done on the famous beaches.

DIRECTIONS ▶ Read each sentence. Write the compound subject and the joining word. In your answer, add commas if they are needed.

1. Sally and John like to take care of their garden.

_____

2. Roses daisies and violets are their favorite flowers.

_____

3. Jim and Meg came over for lunch in the garden.

_____

4. Sally John Jim and Meg sat under the big apple tree.

_____

5. A picnic basket and a jug of lemonade were placed on the blanket.

_____

6. The four friends and their two dogs had a wonderful afternoon.

_____

7. Apples peaches and plums were served for dessert.

_____

8. Frankie and Joanne brought some movies over later.

_____

9. The six friends the two dogs and a few cats went inside after sunset.

_____

Simple Predicates and Complete Predicates

The **simple predicate** is the main word or words in the complete predicate of a sentence.

The **complete predicate** includes all the words that tell what the subject of the sentence is or does.

To locate the simple predicate, find the key word in the complete predicate.

Examples:

Tall, snowcapped mountains <u>reach</u> high into the sky. (simple predicate)

Tall, snowcapped mountains <u>reach high into the sky</u>. (complete predicate)

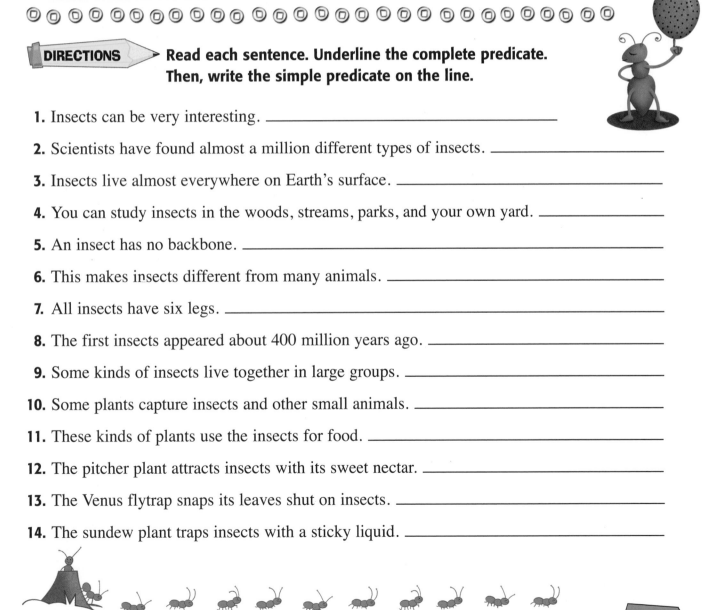

DIRECTIONS ▷ **Read each sentence. Underline the complete predicate. Then, write the simple predicate on the line.**

1. Insects can be very interesting. _____

2. Scientists have found almost a million different types of insects. _____

3. Insects live almost everywhere on Earth's surface. _____

4. You can study insects in the woods, streams, parks, and your own yard. _____

5. An insect has no backbone. _____

6. This makes insects different from many animals. _____

7. All insects have six legs. _____

8. The first insects appeared about 400 million years ago. _____

9. Some kinds of insects live together in large groups. _____

10. Some plants capture insects and other small animals. _____

11. These kinds of plants use the insects for food. _____

12. The pitcher plant attracts insects with its sweet nectar. _____

13. The Venus flytrap snaps its leaves shut on insects. _____

14. The sundew plant traps insects with a sticky liquid. _____

Compound Predicates

A **compound predicate** is two or more predicates that have the same subject. The simple predicates in a compound predicate are usually joined by *and* or *or*.
Examples:

A leopard <u>sprawls</u> along a limb *and* <u>relaxes</u> in a tree.
Bears <u>chase</u> *or* <u>injure</u> sheep sometimes.

DIRECTIONS ▷ **Read each sentence. Write the compound predicate and the joining word. In your answer, add commas if they are needed.**

1. Sandra planned and prepared a surprise party for her sister, Susie.

_____

2. She shopped cleaned and cooked the day before the party.

_____

3. She hired a clown and bought some balloons about a week ahead of time.

_____

4. Four days before the party, Sandra ordered a cake and borrowed extra plates.

_____

5. The guests wore party hats and played party games.

_____

6. Everyone ate laughed and danced.

_____

7. Some of the children cleared the table and helped with the dishes.

_____

8. After the party, the guests walked ran or rode home.

_____

9. After the party, Sandra sat and rested.

_____

Compound Predicates

Complete and Simple Subjects and Predicates

Remember that the complete subject includes all the words that tell whom or what the sentence is about. The simple subject is the main word or words in the complete subject.

The complete predicate includes all the words that tell what the subject of the sentence is or does. The simple predicate is the main word or words in the complete predicate.

DIRECTIONS ➤ Underline each complete subject, and circle each complete predicate. Then, write the simple subject and the simple predicate.

1. Our favorite coach cheers during the race.

_____

2. My youngest sister swims ahead of the others.

_____

3. Her strokes cut through the water.

_____

4. Ripples splash at the edge of the pool.

_____

5. The exciting race ends with a surprise.

_____

6. My sister's team finishes first.

_____

7. The people in the bleachers cheer wildly.

_____

8. The team holds the silver trophy for a school photograph.

_____

9. The team members hug each other happily.

_____

10. Everyone in my family goes for an ice-cream cone.

_____

Simple and Compound Sentences

A sentence that expresses only one complete thought is a **simple sentence**.
A **compound sentence** is made up of two or more simple sentences joined by
a conjunction such as *and, or,* or *but.* Use a comma (,) before a conjunction that
joins two sentences.

Examples:

The family moved to Ohio. (simple sentence)

Patrick liked his new house, and he decided to explore. (compound sentence)

DIRECTIONS ▸ **Read each sentence. Underline each simple subject. Circle each simple predicate. Then, write whether each sentence is a *simple sentence* or a *compound sentence.***

1. Once the house was part of the Underground Railroad, and it had many hiding places.

_____

2. Between 1830 and 1860, the Underground Railroad brought about 50,000 slaves to freedom.

_____

3. Farm wagons were the "trains" on this railroad.

_____

4. Often, the "train rides" were long walks between stations.

_____

5. Runaway slaves stopped at "stations" along the way, but they rarely stayed for long.

_____

6. The home of Frederick Douglass was one "station" on the track to freedom.

_____

7. Levi Coffin was a "conductor" in Indiana, and he earned the title "President of the Underground Railroad."

_____

8. Dies Drear was also a "conductor," but he lived in Ohio.

_____

9. Allan Pinkerton made barrels in Illinois, but he also hid slaves in his shop.

_____

10. Harriet Tubman led slaves to the North, and sometimes she took them to Canada.

_____

Kinds of Sentences

A **declarative sentence** makes a statement or tells something. It ends with a period (.).
An **interrogative sentence** asks a question. It ends with a question mark (?).
An **imperative sentence** makes a request or gives a command. It ends with a period (.). *You* is always the subject of an imperative sentence. Often, the word *you* does not appear in the sentence. It is said to be "understood".
An **exclamatory sentence** shows strong feeling or surprise. It ends with an exclamation point (!).
Examples:

> We are going to see the Statue of Liberty. (declarative)
> Have you ever seen it? (interrogative)
> Come see it with me. (imperative)
> It must be very heavy! (exclamatory)

DIRECTIONS ▷ End each sentence with the correct punctuation mark. Then, write whether the sentence is *declarative, interrogative, imperative,* or *exclamatory*.

1. We are going to New York to see the Statue of Liberty_____

2. We have studied about it in school_____

3. Have you ever seen the Statue of Liberty_____

4. What a feeling it is to be close to her_____

5. Stand over there, and I will take your picture_____

6. It is difficult to imagine that she was a gift_____

7. Can you imagine getting such a large gift_____

8. It would take many mail trucks to deliver it _____

9. We enjoyed our trip to New York this year_____

10. You must go if you get the chance_____

11. Did you know that many New Yorkers have never visited the statue_____

_____

12. Don't be one of those people _____

Subjects in Imperative Sentences

Remember that in an imperative sentence, *you* is always the subject. Often, the word *you* does not appear in the sentence. It is said to be "understood."
Example:
(*You*) Read the directions carefully.

DIRECTIONS ➤ **Read each sentence. Circle each imperative sentence. On the line, write the simple subject of each sentence.**

1. Trash is one of our biggest problems. _____

2. Be very careful with empty cans and bottles. _____

3. Don't just toss them out. _____

4. Put cans and bottles in separate bags. _____

5. The trash problem can be solved. _____

6. Take old newspapers to recycling centers. _____

7. Never toss plastic trash on the ground. _____

8. Pieces of plastic can kill animals. _____

DIRECTIONS ➤ **Change each declarative sentence to an imperative sentence. Write the new sentence on the line.**

9. Packages with too much wrapping should be avoided.

_____

10. People should buy the largest sizes of products.

_____

11. Old T-shirts can be used as wiping rags.

_____

12. Both sides of writing paper can be used.

_____

Agreement of Subjects and Verbs

A verb must agree with its subject in number. Use a singular verb with a singular subject. Use a plural verb with a plural or compound subject.
Examples:

    Chad finds a magic carpet.
    It grants him wishes.
    The *wishes come* true only for Chad.

 **DIRECTIONS** ➤ **Underline the simple subject of each sentence. Then, complete each sentence correctly by circling the form of each verb in ( ) that agrees with the subject.**

1. Chad and his friends (look, looks) around in the old house.

2. Chad (find, finds) an old rug rolled up in a corner.

3. He (pull, pulls) it out and unrolls it.

4. The rug (take, takes) Chad for a ride around the room.

5. Chad's friends (come, comes) into the room as the carpet lands.

6. They (stand, stands) staring with their mouths open.

7. Then, Chad (explain, explains) that the rug has told him he has three wishes.

8. The rug also (tell, tells) Chad that it will take him wherever he wants to go.

9. Chad and his friends (go, goes) for a long ride on the rug.

10. They (fly, flies) over the town and the river.

11. Chad (wish, wishes) that his aunt could come home from the hospital.

12. When Chad gets home, he (hear, hears) his mother talking on the phone.

13. She (says, say) that his aunt can leave the hospital now.

14. In his room, Chad (thank, thanks) the rug and (think, thinks) about his next wishes.

Combining Sentences with the Same Subject or Predicate

A good writer combines two or more sentences that have the same subject or predicate. The conjunctions *and, but,* and *or* are often used to combine sentence parts. When two sentences have the same predicate, the subjects can be combined. *Example:*

> Theseus was angry. King Minos was angry.
> Theseus *and* King Minos were angry.

When two sentences have the same subject, the predicates can be combined. *Example:*

> Theseus found the ring. Theseus returned it.
> Theseus found the ring *and* returned it.

How to Combine Sentences with the Same Subjects or Predicates
1. Find two or more sentences that have the same subject or predicate.
2. Combine the subjects or the predicates with the joining word that most clearly expresses your meaning to the audience.
3. If you combine subjects, make sure you use the plural form of the verb.

 **DIRECTIONS** **Rewrite this paragraph. Combine sentences with the same subjects or predicates to make it more interesting to read.**

Each year, King Minos demanded a human sacrifice from the people of Athens. Seven boys would enter the Labyrinth. Seven girls would enter the Labyrinth. The Labyrinth was the home of the Minotaur. The Minotaur was half man. The Minotaur was half beast.

_____

_____

_____

_____

_____

_____

Combining Adjectives and Adverbs in Sentences

To avoid short, choppy sentences, a writer often combines two or more sentences that describe the same subject. Sentences that describe the same subject with different adjectives can sometimes be combined.
Example:

> Joanie was *diligent*. She was also *courageous*.
> Joanie was *diligent and courageous*.

Sentences that describe the same verb with different adverbs can also be combined.
Example:

> Joanie studied *eagerly*. She studied *carefully*.
> Joanie studied *eagerly and carefully*.

How to Combine Sentences with Adjectives and Adverbs
1. Look for different adjectives or adverbs that describe the same subject or verb.
2. Use an appropriate conjunction (*and, but,* or *or*) to combine the adjectives or the adverbs.
3. If you combine three or more adjectives or adverbs in one sentence, use commas to separate them.

DIRECTIONS ▷ **Combine each set of sentences to make one sentence. Then, tell whether you combined adjectives or adverbs.**

1. Joanie waited patiently. She waited quietly. _____

_____

2. She had felt disappointed before. She had felt rejected before. _____

_____

3. She really wanted to be a scientist. She truly wanted to be a scientist. _____

_____

4. Joanie read the letter slowly. She read the letter calmly. _____

_____

Joining Sentences

A writer can join two short, choppy sentences into one that is more interesting to read. The result is a compound sentence.

Use the conjunction *and* to join two sentences that show addition or similarity.
Example:

> Patrick saw the house. He decided it was haunted.
> Patrick saw the house, *and* he decided it was haunted.

Use the conjunction *but* to join two sentences that show contrast.
Example:

> Patrick ran up the steps. He stopped at the door.
> Patrick ran up the steps, *but* he stopped at the door.

Use the conjunction *or* to join two sentences that show choice.
Example:

> Should he go inside? Should he explore outside?
> Should he go inside, *or* should he explore outside?

How to Combine Sentences
1. Choose two short sentences you want to combine.
2. Select the appropriate conjunction to combine them.
3. Be sure the conjunction makes the meaning of the combined sentence clear.
4. Put a comma before the conjunction.

 **DIRECTIONS** ▸ Join each pair of sentences. Use the conjunctions *and, but,* or *or.*

1. Patrick studied the wall. He found a hidden button.

_____

2. Patrick pushed the button. The bookcase moved.

_____

3. Patrick could wait. He could explore the path.

_____

4. He wasn't afraid. He wasn't comfortable, either.

_____

Sentence Variety

To add variety to sentences, a writer sometimes changes the order of the words. Usually, the subject comes before the verb. This is called **natural order**.
Example:
> Margaret led Danny down a twisting path.

Sometimes the subject and the verb can be reversed. This is called **inverted order**.
Example:
> At the end of the path was a small shack.

How to Vary Word Order in Sentences
1. Choose a sentence you have written in which the subject and the verb can be reversed.
2. Write the sentence in inverted order. Be sure the meaning of the sentence does not change.

 DIRECTIONS ▷ **Write each sentence, changing the word order whenever it would not change the meaning. Tell which sentences cannot be changed and explain why.**

1. On the little door shone the sunlight.

_____

2. Margaret and Danny walked into the shack.

_____

3. Inside the shack was a large wooden table.

_____

4. On the table lay a black cat.

_____

5. Margaret reached out to the cat.

_____

6. At work in the shack was a witch's magic!

_____

7. Margaret told Danny to follow her out.

_____

Avoiding Sentence Fragments and Run-on Sentences

To avoid writing **sentence fragments**, be sure each sentence has a subject and a predicate and expresses a complete thought.

To avoid writing **run-on sentences**, be sure you join two complete sentences with a comma and a conjunction. You may also write them as two separate sentences.

DIRECTIONS ▸ **Read each group of words. If it is a simple sentence, write *simple sentence* on the line. If it is a sentence fragment or a run-on sentence, rewrite it correctly.**

1. A box turtle is a reptile it lives in woods and fields.

_____

2. The box turtle has a hinged lower shell.

_____

3. Can pull its legs, head, and tail inside its shell and get "boxed in."

_____

4. Many kinds of turtles on land and in the water.

_____

5. Belong to the same family as lizards, snakes, alligators, and crocodiles.

_____

_____

6. Box turtles will eat earthworms, insects, berries, and green leafy vegetables.

_____

_____

7. Painted turtles eat meal worms, earthworms, minnows, and insects the musk turtle finds food along the bottoms of ponds or streams.

_____

_____

8. Painted turtles get their name from the red and yellow patterns on their shells they also have yellow lines on their heads.

_____

_____

Correcting Run-on Sentences

Good writers avoid run-on sentences. Run-on sentences may be rewritten as simple sentences or as compound sentences.

DIRECTIONS > **Read each run-on sentence. Fix it in two ways. Write two simple sentences, and write one compound sentence.**

1. You'll need 101 index cards you'll need a colored marker.

a. _____

b. _____

2. Print the name of a state or a state capital on each index card print the rules on the last index card.

a. _____

_____

b. _____

_____

3. Put the marker away put all the cards in an envelope.

a. _____

b. _____

4. This game is for small groups up to three students may play.

a. _____

b. _____

5. Players mix up the cards they lay the cards face down.

a. _____

b. _____

Capitalization of Names and Titles of People and Pets

Begin each part of the name of a person with a capital letter. Capitalize an initial used in a name.

Begin a title of a person, such as *Ms., Mrs., Mr.,* or *Dr.,* with a capital letter.

Always capitalize the word *I*.

Examples:

    Pete P. Pelky

    Mrs. Morrow

    Michael Mixx and I went camping.

DIRECTIONS → **Read each sentence. Circle the letters that should be capital letters.**

1. i was going camping with my friend michael.

2. We met mr. carl g. carbur at the camping supply store.

3. michael and i decided that we needed a new tent.

4. mrs. albright showed us many different tents.

5. we chose one just like dr. pelky's.

6. michael's mother, mrs. mixx, gave us a ride to the campsite.

7. After we set up the tent, i walked down the road.

8. dr. pelky was at the next site!

9. Dr. pelky was camping with mario j. moreno.

10. mario showed michael and me a great place to fish.

11. i caught some trout, and michael caught a bass.

12. michael and i ate supper at dr. pelky's camp.

Capitalization of Proper Nouns and Proper Adjectives

Remember that a proper noun names a particular place, holiday, day of the week, or month. A proper adjective is formed from a proper noun.
Capitalize the first letter of each important word in a proper noun or proper adjective.
Examples:

Canada   Fourth of July   Wednesday   German shepherd

DIRECTIONS → **Rewrite each sentence, using capital letters where needed.**

1. My best friends and i plan to tour the united states.

_____

2. My friend sandy is very excited because she has never been to california.

_____

_____

3. She has never tasted any mexican food, either.

_____

4. She will be coming from new york and meeting jane in philadelphia.

_____

5. Then, the two of them will pick up roxanne in phoenix, arizona.

_____

6. When they get to san francisco, i plan to take them out for chinese food.

_____

_____

7. If we go to green's restaurant for vegetarian food, even jane will like the brussels sprouts.

_____

_____

8. Sometimes i think that july will never get here.

_____

9. I received a letter from sandy last tuesday.

_____

Using Capital Letters

Use a capital letter to begin the first word of a sentence.
Begin each important word in the name of a town, city, state, province, and country with a capital letter.
Begin each important word in the names of streets and their abbreviations with capital letters.
Begin the name of a day of the week or its abbreviation with a capital letter.
Begin the name of a month or its abbreviation with a capital letter.
Examples:
>   Detroit, Michigan
>   Athens, Greece
>   Golden Gate Avenue or Ave.
>   Saturday or Sat.
>   November or Nov.

DIRECTIONS ➤ Rewrite each sentence. Add capital letters where they are needed.

1. i found a book of rhymes at the library in milwaukee.

_____

2. the book was published in london, england.

_____

3. the book contained rhymes from the countries of kenya, ecuador, and even new zealand.

_____

_____

4. my favorite poem told of a crocodile that lived at the corner of cricket court and bee boulevard.

_____

_____

5. we started driving across the painted desert wednesday.

_____

6. thursday morning we saw a beautiful sunrise.

_____

7. we decided to drive to the rocky mountains on sunday.

_____

8. we finally reached el paso, texas, on tuesday.

_____

Periods

Use a **period (.)** at the end of a declarative or imperative sentence.
Use a period after an abbreviation.
Use a period after an initial.
Use a period after the numeral in a main topic and after the capital letter in a subtopic of an outline.
Examples:

Arithmetic adds up to answers.
U.S.   Fri.   Jan.   Dr.   Blvd.
Capt. Chou A. Hak-Tak

I. How to Master Multiplication
    A. Learn multiplication tables
    B. Practice doing multiplication problems

DIRECTIONS ➤ **Correct each item. Add periods where they are needed.**

1. Last week our class visited a Chinese exhibit

2. I thought the pen-and-brush pictures were beautiful

3. I was also impressed with the carved jade ships

4. Our teacher, Ms Garrett, showed us a book about Chinese painting in the museum gift shop

5. The book was written by Dr Chun B Fong.

6. Dr Fong included a chapter about wood-block prints.

7. Our guide, T R Adams, knew all about Chinese art

8. J B Barnard asked several questions.

9. The museum is located on N Clark St

10. I Crafts from China

    A Silk painting

    B Porcelain

Abbreviations and Initials

An **abbreviation** is a short way of writing a word or words.
Begin abbreviations with a capital letter. End most abbreviations with a period.
An **initial** is an abbreviation of a name. The initial is the first letter of the name.
Use capital letters and periods to write an initial.
Examples:

| Doctor = *Dr.* | Road = *Rd.* | Tuesday = *Tues.* |
| August = *Aug.* | Tina Devers = *T. Devers* | |

DIRECTIONS ▸ Rewrite each item. Use the correct abbreviations and initials for the underlined words.

1. My name is <u>Chester Michael</u> Dooley. I live at 4338 Market <u>Boulevard</u> in Alabaster, Alabama. My birthday is on <u>October</u> 27.

_____

_____

2. Suzy <u>Elizabeth</u> Ziegler requests the pleasure of your company at a party in honor of her friend, Maryanne <u>Margaret</u> Marbles. Please come to the country club at 23 Country Club <u>Drive</u> at 4:00 on <u>Tuesday</u>, <u>April</u> 14.

_____

_____

_____

_____

3. The <u>James</u> Harold Calabases take great pride in announcing the birth of their twins, Heather <u>Holly</u> Calabas and <u>James</u> Harold Calabas, <u>Junior</u>. This happy event took place on <u>Monday</u>, <u>August</u> 23, at 3:00.

_____

_____

_____

_____

4. <u>Fortunato Augustus</u> Jones has been appointed assistant to the president of Bags and Boxes, <u>Incorporated</u>. This store is located at 45 Ninety-ninth <u>Avenue</u>.

_____

_____

Using Commas in Sentences

Use a **comma (,)** after the words *yes* and *no* when they begin a statement.
Use commas to separate three or more words in a series.
Use a comma before the word *and, but,* or *or* when two sentences are combined.
Use a comma to separate a word used in direct address from a sentence.
Use a comma between a quotation and the rest of the sentence.
Examples:
> *Yes,* the boys should join their father.
> The boys ran *quickly, silently, and anxiously.*
> Josh felt tired, *but* he continued to run.
> "*Andy,* I need to rest for a minute."
> "*We are almost there,*" said Andy.

DIRECTIONS ▸ Rewrite each sentence, adding commas where they are needed.

1. Three plants to avoid are poison ivy poison oak and poison sumac.

_____

2. "Steven I see that you have some poison oak growing in your yard."

_____

3. "Your dog cat or rabbit can pick it up on its fur and rub against you" Wesley said.

_____

_____

4. Yes it will make your skin burn itch and swell.

_____

5. Dana put his clothes in a hamper and his mother got a rash from touching the clothes.

_____

_____

DIRECTIONS ▸ Cross out any commas that are incorrect. Rewrite the sentence on the line, adding any commas that are needed.

6. Poison ivy looks like, a shrub a vine, or a small plant.

_____

7. Poison ivy, has green leaves in clusters of three and so does poison oak.

_____

_____

Use a comma before the words *and, but,* and *or* in a compound sentence.
Use a comma after time-order words, such as *first, next, then,* and *last.*
Use a comma after introductory words and phrases.
Use a comma to separate three or more words in a series.
Examples:
> The old house was big, *and* it also looked mysterious.
> *First,* I decided to explore the house.
> *Before I had explored very long,* I found a tunnel.
> The tunnel was *dark, damp, and long.*

DIRECTIONS > **Correct each sentence. Put commas where they are needed.**

1. The old house looked interesting but it also looked frightening.

2. I inspected the upstairs and I looked in the backyard.

3. The cellar door was open and I decided to look inside.

4. I could look around in one room or I could go to another room.

5. First I was worried that there was something in the cellar.

6. Next I thought I heard voices coming from the other room.

7. After a while I decided I had better get out of the cellar.

8. In addition I began to remember the stories my mother had told me.

9. I thought of all the other people who had lived played and worked in this house.

10. I imagined that I heard footsteps whispers and singing.

11. I ran out of the cellar and I closed the door behind me.

12. Soon I decided I wanted to explore the upstairs of the house.

More Uses for Commas

Use a comma in an address to separate the city and the state or the city and the country.
Use a comma between the day and the year.
Use a comma after the greeting of a friendly letter and after the closing of any letter.
Examples:

Albuquerque, New Mexico   Lima, Peru
April 30, 2005   Monday, January 27, 2005
Dear Uncle Ernie,
Yours truly,

DIRECTIONS Correct each letter. Add commas where they are needed.

732 Cactus Road
Albuquerque NM 87107
April 22 2005

Dear Ernest
 I need to show Father that I am old enough to go on the summer trail drive. Please help me by reminding Father that I have helped you do many things this year. I will appreciate any help that you can give me.

Your friend

David Ortez

441 Scorpion Trail
Albuquerque NM 87112
May 3 2005

Dear David
 You have helped me a great deal during this past year. I will speak to your father. Remember that your father is a fair man, and he will reward you when he thinks you are ready.

Sincerely

Ernest

Question Marks and Exclamation Points

Use a **question mark (?)** at the end of an interrogative sentence.
Use an **exclamation point (!)** at the end of an exclamatory sentence.
Examples:
> Did Mika know what was in the box?
> What a surprise she received when she reached inside!

DIRECTIONS ➤ **Finish each sentence with a question mark or exclamation point.**

1. Did you know that our teacher, Mr. Holder, visited China last month

2. What a great adventure he had

3. Look at the wonderful postcards he sent our class

4. Do you know where he stayed

5. When did Mr. Holder return

6. Could you tell us about his trip

7. He found a pearl in an oyster shell

8. That was a lucky find

9. You should see the beautiful photographs Mr. Holder took

10. What kind of camera did he use

11. It really is a good one

12. What did he bring back

13. What a beautiful necklace that is

14. Did you know that jade is very expensive

15. Mrs. Holder will certainly be surprised

16. Did Mr. Holder visit the Great Wall of China

17. Of course he did

18. What an awesome sight that must have been

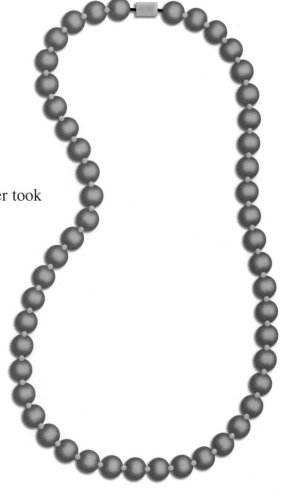

Apostrophes and Colons

Use an **apostrophe (')** to show that one or more letters have been left out in a contraction.

To form a singular possessive noun, add an apostrophe and *s* to singular nouns.

To form a plural possessive noun, add an apostrophe to a plural noun that ends in *s*.

Add an apostrophe and *s* to plural nouns that do not end in *s* to show possession.

Use a **colon (:)** between the hour and the minute in the time of day.

Use a colon after the greeting in a business letter.

Examples:

was not = *wasn't*	could not = *couldn't*
Jane's father	the *pig's* tail
guests' laughter	the *maids'* voices
the *children's* adventure	the *men's* story
2:25 PM	5:13 AM
Dear Ms. Parker:	Dear Sir or Madam:

DIRECTIONS ▷ **Add apostrophes to the following items as needed.**

1. Uncle Chens problem was difficult to explain.

2. The childrens faces lit up when they saw him flying.

3. The boys smiles made Jane laugh.

4. "I cant stop laughing," Jane said.

5. "Wont you join us, Ms. Parker?" Jane asked.

DIRECTIONS ▷ **Add colons to these items as needed.**

6. "It's only 3 30 in the afternoon," Michel said.

7. "We can stay until 6 00," Meri replied.

8. The movie starts at 7 15.

9. Dear Ms. Parker

Your application for employment has been received.

Contractions

A **contraction** is a short way of writing two words together. Some of the letters are left out. An apostrophe takes the place of the missing letters.
Examples:

she + will = *she'll*
had + not = *hadn't*
I + would = *I'd*

DIRECTIONS Rewrite each sentence. Replace the underlined words with a contraction.

1. <u>You are</u> getting very hot in this summer weather.

_____

2. Do you think <u>you would</u> like a water slide?

_____

3. <u>You will</u> need some plastic at least ten feet long.

_____

4. <u>It is</u> best to get heavy plastic.

_____

5. That way, it <u>will not</u> tear too easily.

_____

6. Place the plastic on a grassy spot where there <u>are not</u> any bumps.

_____

_____

7. You can use stones to hold the plastic down, but they <u>must not</u> be sharp.

_____

_____

8. If you <u>do not</u> have a sprinkler, get one.

_____

9. You <u>should not</u> put the sprinkler too far from the plastic.

_____

10. You <u>must not</u> let the plastic get dry.

_____

Direct Quotations and Dialogue

Use a **direct quotation** to tell a speaker's exact words.
Use **quotation marks (" ")** before and after the words a speaker says.
Begin the first word a speaker says with a capital letter. Put end punctuation before the ending quotation marks. Begin a new paragraph each time the speaker changes.
If the quotation is interrupted by other words, place quotation marks around the exact spoken words only.
Examples:

Dad asked, "Where have you been?"
"I went to the store," Vic said. "Then, I went to the library."

DIRECTIONS ➤ Write quotation marks where they are needed in the following sentences.

1. Have you heard of the Nobel Peace Prize? asked Emi.

2. Yes. Mother Teresa and Nelson Mandela have won it, replied Jan.

3. But do you know who Nobel was? Emi asked.

4. Jan responded, No, I guess I don't.

5. He invented dynamite, stated Emi.

6. It seems weird, said Jan, to name a peace prize for the inventor of dynamite.

7. In fact, Emi said, dynamite was once called Nobel's Safety Blasting Powder.

8. Nobel patented the blasting powder in 1867, Emi continued.

9. He did not want dynamite used for war, he said.

10. He added, Nobel once said that war is the horror of horrors and the greatest of all crimes.

11. How did the Nobel Prizes get started? asked Jan.

12. Emi said, In his will, Nobel said that his money should be used to establish prizes in five areas: physics, chemistry, medicine, literature, and peace.

13. Sometimes a prize is shared by two or three people, he continued.

14. I'd like to know more about some of the winners, Jan said.

15. Jimmy Carter, the 39th president of the United States, won the Nobel Peace Prize in 2002, replied Emi.

Titles

Underline the titles of books, newspapers, magazines, movies, and television shows.
If you are using a computer to write, replace underlining with italics.
Use quotation marks around the titles of stories, magazine articles, essays, songs, or poems.
Begin the first word, last word, and all other important words in a title with a capital letter.
Examples:

<u>I Like Frogs</u> (book)
<u>Shrek</u> (movie)
"Wind in the Treetops" (story)
"The Bells" (poem)

DIRECTIONS > **Write each title. Use capital letters correctly. Underline or use quotation marks as needed.**

1. a wrinkle in time (book) _____

2. camping in the mountains (magazine article) _____

3. it's not easy being green (song) _____

4. sounder (movie) _____

5. the new york times (newspaper) _____

6. humpty dumpty (magazine) _____

7. the little house (story) _____

8. why i like gymnastics (essay) _____

9. the little prince (book) _____

10. the owl and the pussycat (poem) _____

DIRECTIONS > **Rewrite each sentence correctly.**

11. The sixth chapter in that book is called Animal Language.

_____

12. A book I really like is If I Were in Charge of the World by Judith Viorst.

_____

_____

Compound Words

A **compound word** consists of two or more words used as a single word.
A **closed compound** is a compound made of two words written together as one.
Examples:

runway   bookmark   rainbow

An **open compound** is a compound in which the words are written separately.
Examples:

dead end   punching bag   bean sprout

A **hyphenated compound** is a compound connected by hyphens.
Examples:

father-in-law   half-truth   narrow-minded

DIRECTIONS There are eighteen compounds in the following sentences, but all of them are spelled incorrectly. Identify each compound, and spell it correctly. Use a dictionary if necessary. Then, write each word correctly.

1. My cousin Danielle had her wisdom-teeth pulled. _____

2. As she sat in an arm chair in the sun-shine, she thought about an old family story.

_____

3. Isaac, a ten year-old boy, had escaped from slavery. _____

4. His spirits soared skyhigh as he left his birth place. _____

5. The slavedriver went after him with blood-hounds. _____

6. Isaac hid in a stormcellar and a smoke house as he headed north to freedom.

_____

7. For three weeks he lived handtomouth, but he avoided any run ins with his former master.

_____

8. Danielle, a folk-singer of sorts, reached for her note book.

_____

9. "This is no run of the mill story," she thought as she gazed at the wall-paper.

_____

10. "This old story from our familytree will make a terrific song or even a best selling novel!"

_____

Synonyms and Antonyms

A **synonym** is a word that has almost the same meaning as another word.
When a word has several synonyms, use the one that works best in the sentence.
An **antonym** is a word that means the opposite of another word.
When a word has more than one antonym, use the one that expresses your meaning exactly.
Examples:

  Jobs is a synonym of *tasks*.
  Short is an antonym of *tall*.

DIRECTIONS   Read each sentence. Study the underlined words. Then, write *synonyms* or *antonyms* to describe the two words.

1. As Tio and Nicole approached the <u>forest</u>, they saw a path leading into the <u>woods</u>.

   _____

2. The trees were dripping with moisture, and soon Tio's and Nicole's <u>dry</u> clothes were <u>soaked</u>.

   _____

3. Within the forest, the <u>upper</u> branches kept the light from reaching the <u>lower</u> levels.

   _____

4. As they walked along the muddy <u>path</u>, Tio and Nicole saw rotting leaves on the <u>trail</u>.

   _____

5. They <u>continued</u> along the trail and then <u>halted</u> suddenly in their tracks.

   _____

6. The <u>low</u> sound of a <u>soft</u> chirping had caused them to stop.

   _____

7. As they moved <u>quietly</u> through the forest, they heard a monkey <u>loudly</u> calling to other monkeys.

   _____

8. The <u>younger</u> monkeys were eating leaves of bamboo trees while the <u>older</u> ones watched.

   _____

9. One monkey was <u>curious</u> and looked at Tio and Nicole, but the others were <u>indifferent</u>.

   _____

More Synonyms and Antonyms

Remember that a synonym is a word that has almost the same meaning as another word. An antonym is a word that means the opposite of another word.
Examples:

      Start is a synonym of *begin.*
      Hard is an antonym of *soft.*

DIRECTIONS   **Read each sentence. Identify the two words or two phrases from the sentence that are antonyms, and write them on the lines.**

1. Barbra had always been a success at school, but now she felt like a failure.

    _____   _____

2. T. J. had been left back once because he wasn't mature enough to be promoted.

    _____   _____

3. Barbra saw only one solution to her problem—she had to get rid of her report card.

    _____   _____

4. Barbra had a burning feeling in her stomach that even ice-cold milk couldn't get rid of.

    _____   _____

DIRECTIONS   **Fill in the columns of the chart with a synonym and an antonym for each of the words in the first column.**

Word	Synonym	Antonym
end	_____	_____
fast	_____	_____
simple	_____	_____
gloomy	_____	_____
concealed	_____	_____
unsure	_____	_____

Prefixes

A **prefix** is a letter or group of letters added to the beginning of a base word. A **base word** is the simplest form of a word.
Adding a prefix to a word changes the word's meaning.
Examples:
dis + like = dislike
The boys said they *like* being in the cave.
They *dislike* the cold rocks.

DIRECTIONS ▸ Find the word in each sentence that begins with a prefix. Draw a line under the prefix. Then, write a definition of the word.

1. There may be gold in the Black Mountains, waiting to be unearthed.

   _____

2. Many people say this gold is nonexistent.

   _____

3. Others say it's there, but they are unable to find it.

   _____

4. Many searches for the gold have had to be discontinued.

   _____

5. It is improbable that any gold is there.

   _____

6. Our inability to find any probably means there is none.

   _____

DIRECTIONS ▸ On the line, write a word with the meaning given in ( ). Use one of the prefixes in the box, and use the underlined word as a base word.

dis	mis	pre	re	un	non	in	im

7. I bought it last week, but I will _____ (<u>sell</u> again) it to you.

8. I have never been _____ (not <u>sincere</u>) with you.

9. I sense some _____ (opposite of <u>comfort</u>) in you.

10. Have you ever known me to _____ (<u>lead</u> incorrectly) you?

11. You don't even have to _____ (<u>pay</u> before) me for the map.

12. I'm a little _____ (not <u>organized</u>) now, but I'll get the map to you tomorrow.

Suffixes

A **suffix** is a letter or group of letters added to the ending of a base word.
A **base word** is a word to which other word parts may be added.
A suffix changes the meaning of a word.
Example:

> Do you get *enjoyment* from reading Greek myths, or do they *frighten* you?

Sometimes spelling changes are made when suffixes are added to base words. Drop the *e* at the end of a base word before adding a suffix that begins with a vowel.
Examples:

> contribute—contributor   love—lovable

Noun-forming Suffixes		Adjective-forming Suffixes		Verb-forming Suffix	
Suffix	Example	Suffix	Example	Suffix	Example
er	singer	able	laughable	en	brighten
or	director	ful	careful		
ness	gentleness	ible	flexible	**Adverb-forming Suffix**	
ment	appointment	ish	selfish	Suffix	Example
		less	careless	ly	quickly
		y	stormy		

DIRECTIONS ▷ **Add the kind of suffix given in ( ) to each word. Then, on a separate sheet of paper, write a sentence with each word you have formed.**

1. sail (noun) _____

2. fear (adjective) _____

3. kind (noun) _____

4. might (adjective) _____

5. happy (noun) _____

6. light (verb) _____

7. cloud (adjective) _____

8. sudden (adverb) _____

9. quiet (adverb) _____

10. play (noun, adjective) _____

11. wonder (adjective) _____

12. teach (noun) _____

Homophones and Homographs

Homophones are words that sound alike but are spelled differently and have different meanings.
Example:
> The girl *read* the *red* sign.

Homographs are words that have the same spelling but different meanings. Some homographs are pronounced differently.
Examples:
> Some animals *live* on land and water.
> *Live* plants are not allowed in this building.

 **DIRECTIONS** Read each sentence. Circle the homophone in ( ) that correctly completes the sentence.

1. Leaves need (air, heir) in order to breathe.

2. If plants can't breathe, then neither can (ewe, you).

3. Of (coarse, course), if we keep cutting down trees, we'll have less oxygen.

4. It (wood, would) be a mistake to put a plant right next to a heater.

5. Most plants (need, knead) the temperature to be kept even.

6. The (main, mane) enemy of most plants is dry heat.

7. You should spray your plants with a fine (missed, mist) of warm water every day.

 **DIRECTIONS** Use one of the following homographs to complete each sentence.

object	can	present	spring

8. If you mix your own plant food, you _____ do it in a _____.

9. If you _____ to putting a plant in a bigger pot, remember the _____ of replanting.

10. To give your crowded plant a nice _____, _____ it with a bigger pot.

11. In the _____, many plants grow by the _____ in the forest.

More on Homophones

Remember that homophones are words that sound alike. They are spelled differently and have different meanings.
Example:
>Brandon spent *four* days thinking about a gift *for* his friend Cara.

DIRECTIONS ▶ **Complete each sentence. Choose the correct homophone in ( ). Write it on the line.**

1. At the end of the _____, Brandon chose a plan.
(week, weak)

2. He made his _____ to the bus station and traveled downtown.
(way, weigh)

3. The sporting goods store was easy to _____.
(fined, find)

4. Brandon thought, "I _____ what Cara would like."
(know, no)

5. "This is what I have to _____."
(dew, do)

6. Could he get _____ the line to get an autograph?
(threw, through)

7. Brandon could _____ his hero.
(see, sea)

8. His heart _____ faster.
(beet, beat)

9. Cara would get _____ special baseball from Brandon.
(won, one)

DIRECTIONS ▶ **Write one homophone for each of the following words. Then, use five pairs of homophones correctly in sentences. Spell each homophone correctly. Use a separate sheet of paper.**

10. pail _____

11. son _____

12. flea _____

13. strait _____

14. two _____

15. meet _____

16. led _____

17. sighed _____

18. blew _____

19. hymn _____

20. pane _____

21. hoarse _____

Words with Multiple Meanings

Some words have more than one meaning. When you read something, you need to be sure you know which meaning the writer intends.

DIRECTIONS ▷ Look at the words and their meanings in the chart. Then, read each sentence below, and select the appropriate meaning for the underlined word. Write it in the space provided.

Word	Meanings	
sail	a. cloth that catches wind to move a boat	b. to move in a boat
craft	a. a skill or an occupation	b. a ship, boat, or aircraft
mission	a. something a person sets out to do	b. a religious outpost
passed	a. moved past or went by	b. voted in favor of, approved
named	a. appointed to a job or an office	b. gave a name to
reached	a. stretched one's hand or arm out	b. arrived at or came to
completed	a. made whole with nothing missing	b. ended or finished

1. Ferdinand Magellan was the first explorer to <u>sail</u> around the world.

In this sentence, *sail* means _____.

2. His <u>craft</u> had to travel from Spain across the Atlantic to South America.

In this sentence, *craft* means _____.

3. From there his <u>mission</u> was to sail along the eastern shore until he reached the southernmost tip.

In this sentence, *mission* means _____.

4. Magellan <u>passed</u> through a strait now named for him and found a great ocean.

In this sentence, *passed* means _____.

5. He <u>named</u> this great ocean the Pacific Ocean, which means "peaceful ocean."

In this sentence, *named* means _____.

6. Magellan continued sailing across the Pacific Ocean and <u>reached</u> the Philippine Islands.

In this sentence, *reached* means _____.

7. After Magellan's death, his crew sailed on and <u>completed</u> the historic voyage around the world.

In this sentence, *completed* means _____.

Troublesome Words

Use *too* when you mean "very" or "also." Use *to* when you mean "in the direction of." Use *two* when you mean the numeral 2.

Use *it's* when you mean "it is." Use *its* when you mean "belonging to it."

Use *their* when you mean "belonging to them." Use *there* when you mean "in that place." Use *they're* when you mean "they are."

Use *your* when you mean "belonging to you." Use *you're* when you mean "you are."

The word *good* is an adjective. Use *good* to describe a noun. Use *well* as an adjective when you mean "healthy." Use *well* as an adverb when you tell how something is done.

DIRECTIONS > **Circle the word in ( ) that correctly completes each sentence.**

1. We went (to, too, two) the aquarium.

2. Len stayed home because he did not feel (good, well).

3. (Its, It's) a great place to visit.

4. You forgot to bring (you're, your) lunch.

5. (To, Too, Two) beluga whales were (there, their, they're).

6. One whale had a cute spot on (its, it's) face.

7. (You're, Your) the first person I told about our trip.

8. I wish you had been able to come, (to, too, two).

9. It was a (good, well) idea to take the trip.

10. (There, Their, They're) very happy to have students visit them.

11. The fish and other sea animals are taken care of (good, well).

12. We saw the sea otters eat (there, their, they're) meal.

13. I think (its, it's) worthwhile to go again.

14. Did you see the (to, too, two) walruses?

15. (There, Their, They're) sea lions, not walruses.

Negatives

A **negative** is a word that means "no" or "not."
The words *never, no, nobody, none, not, nothing,* and *nowhere* are negatives.
The negative word *not* is often used in contractions.
Do not use two negatives in the same sentence. This is called a double negative.
Examples:
> Jack had *never* worked in a store before.
> *Nobody* there knew him.
> He *didn't* know at first what he should do.

DIRECTIONS > Complete each sentence by choosing the correct word in ( ). Avoid using two negatives in the same sentence.

1. Most people _____ never get a snakebite.
(will, won't)

2. If you do get bitten, don't go into _____ panic.
(a, no)

3. Remember that not all snakes _____ poisonous.
(are, aren't)

4. It's best not to do _____ that will speed the spread of the poison.
(anything, nothing)

5. Didn't _____ in our group ever study this before?
(anybody, nobody)

6. If you must go for help, don't _____ run.
(ever, never)

7. When in snake country, don't take _____ chances.
(any, no)

DIRECTIONS > Each sentence contains a double negative. Cut or replace at least one of the negatives. Write the sentence correctly.

8. There aren't no more than four kinds of poisonous snakes in North America.

_____

_____

9. It won't do no good to try to run away from a rattlesnake.

_____

Avoiding Wordy Language

Good writers say what they mean in as few words as possible. When you revise, cross out words that don't add to the meaning.

Example:

> *Mari was putting on her clothes and getting ready for Chet's party.* (wordy)
> *Mari was dressing for Chet's party.* (better)

DIRECTIONS ➤ **Rewrite each sentence. Replace the words in ( ) with fewer words.**

1. Our family was (putting clothes and other items in) suitcases.

_____

2. Everyone was looking forward to (the vacation that we take every year).

_____

3. When all the suitcases were packed, Mom (put all the suitcases in) the trunk.

_____

4. We (pulled out of the driveway) at noon on Saturday.

_____

5. We (made our way through the streets) to the freeway.

_____

6. We (ended up stopping every little while) because my little brother was (not feeling very well).

_____

7. The first day of travel seemed (to go pretty well), though.

_____

8. The second day we (stopped off and went to see the sights of) historical places.

_____

9. Everyone (really had a good time on) the rest of the trip, too.

_____

10. (Each one of our neighbors) welcomed us back.

_____

Using Sensory Images

Good writers use sensory words that appeal to some or all of the five senses.
Example:
  Cold, white snow blanketed the *green pine trees* in the *quiet valley.*

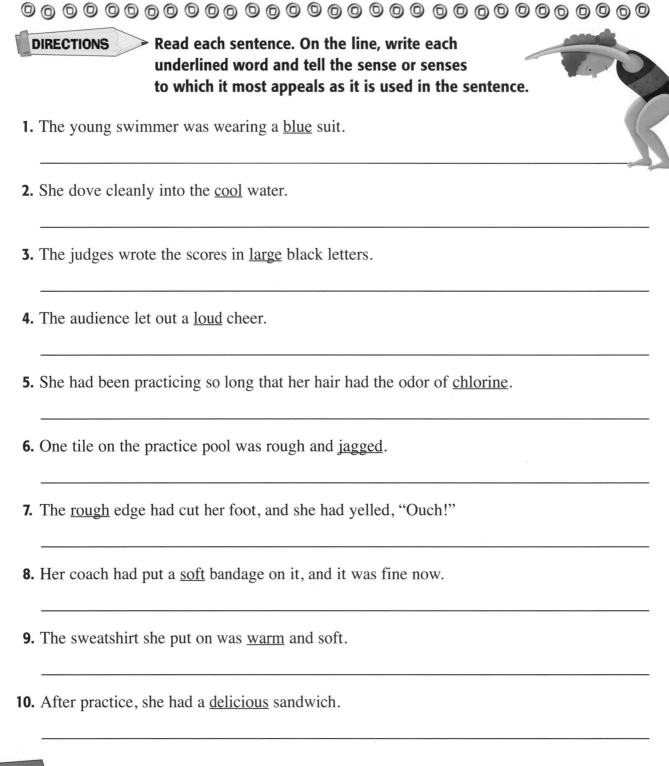

DIRECTIONS ➤ **Read each sentence. On the line, write each underlined word and tell the sense or senses to which it most appeals as it is used in the sentence.**

1. The young swimmer was wearing a <u>blue</u> suit.

_____

2. She dove cleanly into the <u>cool</u> water.

_____

3. The judges wrote the scores in <u>large</u> black letters.

_____

4. The audience let out a <u>loud</u> cheer.

_____

5. She had been practicing so long that her hair had the odor of <u>chlorine</u>.

_____

6. One tile on the practice pool was rough and <u>jagged</u>.

_____

7. The <u>rough</u> edge had cut her foot, and she had yelled, "Ouch!"

_____

8. Her coach had put a <u>soft</u> bandage on it, and it was fine now.

_____

9. The sweatshirt she put on was <u>warm</u> and soft.

_____

10. After practice, she had a <u>delicious</u> sandwich.

_____

Denotation and Connotation

The **denotation** of a word is its exact meaning as stated in a dictionary. Denotations use literal language.

The **connotation** of a word is a second, suggested meaning of a word. This added meaning often suggests something positive or negative. Connotations use figurative language.

Examples:

    Skinny suggests "too thin." *Skinny* has a negative connotation.
    Slender suggests "attractively thin." *Slender* has a positive connotation.

Some words are neutral. They do not suggest either good or bad meanings. For example, *hat, seventeen,* and *yearly* are neutral words.

DIRECTIONS ▷ **Circle the word in ( ) that has the more positive connotation.**

1. Our trip to the amusement park was (good, wonderful).

2. (Brave, foolhardy) people rode on the roller coaster.

3. We saw (fascinating, weird) animals in the animal house.

4. Some of the monkeys made (hilarious, goofy) faces.

5. Everyone's face wore a (smile, smirk) on the way home.

DIRECTIONS ▷ **Circle the word in ( ) that has the more negative connotation.**

6. We bought (cheap, inexpensive) souvenirs at the park.

7. I ate a (soggy, moist) sandwich.

8. Mike (nagged, reminded) us to go to the fun house.

9. He was very (determined, stubborn) about going.

10. The fun house was (comical, silly).

DIRECTIONS ▷ **Answer the following questions.**

11. Which is more serious, a <u>problem</u> or a <u>disaster</u>?

_____

12. Which is worth more, something <u>old</u> or something <u>antique</u>?

_____

Denotation and Connotation, page 2

Remember, the denotation of a word is its exact meaning as stated in a dictionary. The connotation of a word is an added meaning that suggests something positive or negative.

Some words, such as *hat, seventeen,* or *yearly*, are neutral. They do not suggest either good or bad meanings.

Examples:

The denotation of *stingy* is "not generous" or "miserly."

Stingy suggests "selfish." *Stingy* has a negative connotation.

DIRECTIONS ▸ **Read each sentence. Write *negative* if the underlined word has a negative connotation. Write *positive* if it has a positive connotation. Write *neutral* if the word is neutral.**

_____ 1. This is my <u>house</u>.

_____ 2. This is my <u>home</u>.

_____ 3. Darren's friends <u>discussed</u> his problem.

_____ 4. Darren's friends <u>gossiped</u> about his problem.

_____ 5. Our dog is <u>sick</u>.

_____ 6. Our dog is <u>diseased</u>.

_____ 7. The play was <u>boring</u>.

_____ 8. The play was <u>fantastic</u>.

_____ 9. Angie was <u>stubborn</u>.

_____ 10. Angie was <u>determined</u>.

DIRECTIONS ▸ **Complete each sentence with a word that suggests the connotation given.**

11. The gift from my aunt was _____. (positive)

12. The gift from my aunt was _____. (negative)

13. The gift from my aunt was _____. (neutral)

Using Figurative Language

Writers often use **figurative language** to compare unlike things. Figurative language uses figures of speech such as similes, metaphors, and personification. Figurative language gives a meaning that is not exactly that of the words used. Figurative language tries to create a clearer word picture for the reader.

Writers can create vivid word pictures by comparing two things that are not usually thought of as being alike. When *like* or *as* is used to compare two things, the comparison is called a **simile**. A **metaphor** makes a comparison by speaking of one thing as if it were another.

Sometimes a writer will give human characteristics to nonhuman things. Objects, ideas, places, or animals may be given human qualities. They may perform human actions. This kind of language is called **personification**.
Examples:

> *His feet* smelled <u>like</u> *dead fish.* (simile)
> *Paul Bunyan* was as big <u>as</u> a *tree.* (simile)
> The deep *lake* was a *golden mirror* reflecting the setting Sun. (metaphor)
> The old tree moaned with pain in the cold wind. (personification)

DIRECTIONS ▶ **The sentences below include figurative language. Rewrite each sentence. Express the same idea without using figurative language.**

1. I was as jumpy as a cat in a roomful of rocking chairs.

_____

2. As I looked out over the audience, my heart was a brick in my chest.

_____

3. I touched the piano keys, and my fingers were like fence posts.

_____

4. Luckily for me, the performance was as smooth as silk.

_____

5. The last notes whispered, "You did just fine!"

_____

DIRECTIONS ▶ **Complete each sentence below by using figurative language.**

6. The deserted old house was as dark as _____ .

7. When I opened the squeaky front door, it creaked _____ .

Using Figurative Language, page 2

Remember that writers often use figurative language to compare unlike things. Figurative language uses figures of speech such as similes, metaphors, and personification. Figurative language gives a meaning that is not exactly that of the words used.

DIRECTIONS ▷ **Read the paragraph below. Notice how the author uses figurative language to help you visualize the events and descriptions. Then, answer the questions.**

Riding as fast as the wind, Sir Garland spurred his horse toward the castle. When he dashed across the open field, his shadow rode beside him like a good friend. When he galloped through the forest, the leaves whispered, "Hurry! Hurry!" The branches were enemies that caught at his sleeves. Sir Garland rounded a bend, and there before him was the castle, its glistening walls shining more brightly than the sun. "I must see the king!" Sir Garland shouted to the guards. "I bring the most important news in all the world!"

1. What comparison shows how fast Sir Garland was riding?

_____

2. What human characteristic did the author give to the leaves?

_____

3. What simile describes Sir Garland's shadow?

_____

4. What metaphor describes the branches?

_____

DIRECTIONS ▷ **Write three sentences using figurative language.**

5. _____

6. _____

7. _____

Paragraphs

A **paragraph** is a group of sentences that tells about one main idea. The first line of a paragraph is indented. This means the first word is moved in a little from the left margin.

The **topic sentence** expresses the main idea of the paragraph. It tells what all the other sentences in the paragraph are about. The topic sentence is often the first sentence in a paragraph.

The other sentences in a paragraph are **detail sentences.** Detail sentences add information about the topic sentence. They help the audience understand more about the main idea.

Example:

   Optical illusions occur when your eyes and brain give you the wrong idea about the way something looks. In one kind of optical illusion, the brain compares the images you see to images in your memory. Then, your brain makes the wrong interpretation about the new image. Another optical illusion takes place when the brain cannot choose between equally possible interpretations. In yet another, the brain works perfectly well. However, the bending of light through the atmosphere creates mirages that fool your eyes.

How to Write a Paragraph

1. Write a topic sentence that clearly tells the main idea of your paragraph.
2. Indent the first line.
3. Write detail sentences that tell about the main idea.

 **DIRECTIONS**   **Complete this chart with details from the example paragraph.**

Main Idea: _____

Detail: _____

Detail: _____

Detail: _____

Keeping to the Topic

Good writers keep to the point when they give information. Good writers make sure that each paragraph has a topic sentence and that every other sentence in the paragraph is about the topic sentence. Good writers plan a paragraph so that it gives details about one main idea.

DIRECTIONS ▷ **Circle the letter of the sentence that keeps to the topic in the numbered sentence.**

1. Indira Gandhi was an important leader in India during this century.

   a. John Kennedy was an important leader in the United States.

   b. In 1980, she was elected prime minister of India for the third time.

2. Indira Gandhi believed strongly in women's rights.

   a. She once said, "If a woman has the qualifications and ability for any profession, she should be in it."

   b. Her second son, Sanjay, was born in 1946.

3. When Indira was 12 years old, she organized other children in the "Monkey Brigade."

   a. Indira's father was Jawaharlal Nehru.

   b. The Monkey Brigade was very helpful to the Congress.

4. The Monkey Brigade took over many kinds of tasks from the Congress.

   a. They became good at cooking and serving food, making flags, and stuffing envelopes.

   b. Indira Gandhi lived for almost 67 years.

DIRECTIONS ▷ **Draw a line through any sentences that are not about the topic sentence (the first sentence in the paragraph).**

India's famous "March to the Sea" or "Salt March" was led by Mohandas K. Gandhi. My mother went to India last year. At that time, the British did not allow Indians to make their own salt. Not only that, they had to buy their salt from British merchants. Cinnamon and ginger come from India. To defy this unfair law, Gandhi marched 200 miles to the sea, picking up thousands of Indians along the way. The Ganges is a river in India. Once there, Gandhi took a handful of salt from the beach. From that day onward, people all over India began to gather salt themselves.

Connecting a Main Idea and Details

In an **expository paragraph**, good writers express the main idea in a well-focused topic sentence. They connect the details and examples in the paragraph to the topic sentence and to each other.

DIRECTIONS These four sentences can be arranged as a paragraph. Write *M* for main idea or *D* for detail to identify each sentence.

_____ **1.** September 7 is Brazil's Independence Day.

_____ **2.** This holiday celebrates Brazil's independence from Portugal.

_____ **3.** The green and yellow colors of Brazil's flag are everywhere.

_____ **4.** People wear green and yellow T-shirts.

DIRECTIONS Read the sentences. Use the graphic organizer to arrange the main idea and the details.

Other products of these new factories include shoes, textiles, construction equipment, and leather products. Some of these manufacturing plants produce cars, trucks, and farm equipment. Many large factories have been built in southern Brazil. Many of the goods produced in the factories of southern Brazil are shipped to the United States.

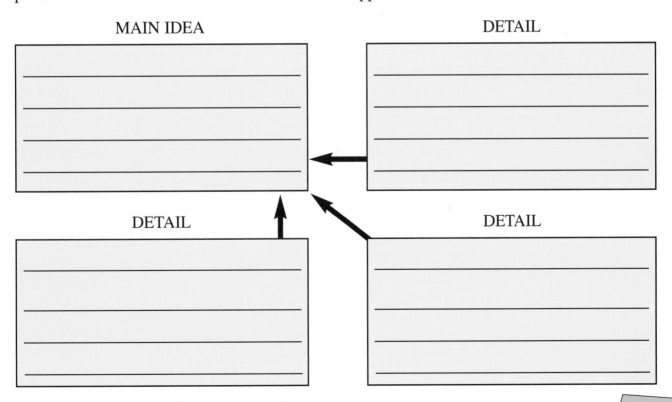

MAIN IDEA

DETAIL

DETAIL

DETAIL

Using Details to Explain

Good writers include details that give causes and effects. They tell their feelings in response to certain causes.

DIRECTIONS ▶ The numbered sentences tell about events. After each numbered sentence, write the detail sentence from the box that helps explain that event.

He was already an expert rider.
The Crow Indians had stolen some Sioux horses.
Slow had jabbed the Crow with his stick.
He no longer seemed so slow and serious.
He had a slow and serious nature.
It was considered braver to push an enemy
  off a horse than to shoot an arrow from far away.
Slow had acted bravely.
They had won the battle.

1. When Sitting Bull was a child, he was named Slow. _____

_____

2. At the age of ten, Slow was given his own pony. _____

_____

3. When Slow was fourteen, he and other Sioux fought some Crow Indians. _____

_____

4. Slow was armed only with a stick. _____

_____

5. One Crow Indian fell from his horse. _____

_____

6. The Sioux held a victory party. _____

_____

Narrative

A **narrative** is a story. It tells about real or made-up events. A narrative tells about one main idea. A narrative should have a beginning, a middle, and an end. Most narratives have **dialogue**. A writer uses dialogue to show how characters speak to one another.

Example:

A Gleam in the Dust

Marc Haynes sadly waved good-bye to his friend Thomas and began to walk home. As he was walking, he saw something gleaming in the dirt. He bent over and picked up a coin. Then he read the date, and his eyes opened wide. The date on the coin was 1789!

Marc took the coin to Mr. Ortiz at the coin shop. "Well, Marc," Mr. Ortiz said, "this is a rare coin you've found. It was stolen from a private collection. I know that the owner is offering a reward of fifty dollars for the return of this coin."

Marc ran all the way home. "Wow!" he thought to himself. "I don't even have to leave town like Thomas did to have an adventure!"

How to Write a Story and Dialogue
1. Write an interesting beginning to present the main character and the setting.
2. Tell about a problem that the main character has to solve in the middle. Tell about what happens in order.
3. Write an ending. Tell how the main character solves the problem or meets the challenge.
4. Write a title for your story.
5. Place quotation marks before and after a speaker's exact words.
6. Use a comma to separate a quotation from the rest of the sentence unless a question mark or exclamation point is needed.
7. Begin a new paragraph each time the speaker changes.
8. Be sure the conversation sounds like real people talking. Use words that tell exactly how the character speaks.

Narrative, page 2

DIRECTIONS ▶ **Read the example narrative at the top of page 93. Then, answer the questions.**

1. What is the problem in the narrative?

_____

_____

2. How is the problem solved?

_____

_____

3. Which two characters have dialogue?

_____

_____

DIRECTIONS ▶ **Think about a story that you would like to tell. Use the graphic organizer to plan your narrative.**

WRITING PLAN

Beginning	Middle	End
Characters: Setting:	Problem:	Solution:

Narrative, page 3

Tips for Writing a Narrative
- Think about an exciting story to tell your reader.
- Create a realistic setting and at least three characters.
- Organize your ideas into a beginning, a middle, and an end.
- Write an interesting introduction that "grabs" your readers.
- Write a believable ending for your story.

DIRECTIONS Think about a story you would like to tell the readers. Use your writing plan as a guide for writing your narrative.

_____

_____

_____

_____

_____

_____

_____

_____

_____

_____

_____

_____

_____

_____

_____

_____

_____

Descriptive Paragraph

In a **descriptive paragraph**, a writer describes a person, place, thing, or event. A good description lets the reader see, feel, hear, and sometimes taste or smell what is being described.

Example:

> Thanksgiving has to be my favorite holiday. The delicious aromas of turkey roasting and pumpkin pies baking fill the house. The lovely autumn colors of orange, gold, red, and brown can be seen in the special flower arrangements for the table. The sound of children laughing as they play games outside mixes with the music being played inside. The sights, smells, and sounds are very important to me.

How to Write a Descriptive Paragraph
1. Write a topic sentence that clearly tells what the paragraph is about.
2. Add detail sentences that give exact information about your topic.
3. Use colorful and lively words to describe the topic. Make an exact picture for the reader with the words you choose.

DIRECTIONS ▷ Complete this paragraph. Add descriptive words that appeal to your senses. Then, in the ( ), tell to what sense each descriptive word appeals.

One _____ (_____) night we went to Loch Ness to see Nessie. We all wore _____ (_____) sweaters and gloves because of the _____ (_____) air. The sun set beyond the Loch, dropping like an _____ (_____) ball. _____ (_____) chirps interrupted the quiet. A _____ (_____) fog settled around us and made our clothes seem _____ (_____). Before we knew it, the _____ (_____) sun had appeared, but we had not seen Nessie.

Descriptive Paragraph, page 2

DIRECTIONS ▷ Read the example description at the top of page 96. Then, answer the questions.

1. What is the writer describing in the paragraph?

_____

2. What is the topic sentence?

_____

3. What are some words the writer uses that appeal to your senses?

_____

_____

_____

DIRECTIONS ▷ Think about something that you would like to describe. It could be a thing, a person you know, or something that has happened to you. Write it in the circle. Then, write words on the lines that describe your topic. Use the graphic organizer to plan your descriptive paragraph.

WRITING PLAN

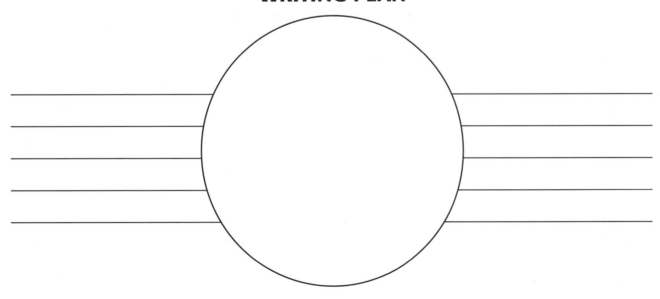

Descriptive Paragraph, page 3

Tips for Writing a Descriptive Paragraph
- Describe a person, a place, an object, or an event.
- Paint a picture using words.
- Use words that appeal to the reader's senses. Let the reader see, smell, taste, feel, and hear what you are writing about.
- Include a sentence that introduces your topic.
- Write detail sentences that use descriptive words.

DIRECTIONS Think about something that you would like to describe. Introduce your topic in your first sentence. Then, use the words that you wrote in the graphic organizer to describe it. Be sure to appeal to the reader's senses.

_____

_____

_____

_____

_____

_____

_____

_____

_____

_____

_____

_____

_____

_____

_____

_____

Business Letter

In a **business letter,** a writer usually writes to someone he or she does not know. One purpose of a business letter is to ask for information or to place an order for something.

A friendly letter has five parts: a heading, a greeting, a body, a closing, and a signature. In addition to the five parts of a friendly letter, a business letter has an inside address. It is the receiver's address.

Example:

heading —
1492 Nakajama Road
Franklin, TN 37064
October 16, 2005

Felicia T. Azar, President
Department of Parks and Recreation
1633 Alberta Place
Franklin, TN 37064
— **inside address**

greeting — Dear Ms. Azar:

body —
    I am writing to suggest that the soft-drink machines in the park be removed. In their place, I recommend that fresh fruit machines be installed. There are two reasons I think this is a good idea. First, soft drinks have too much sugar in them, and they have no nutritional value. Second, with soft-drink machines, the city has the problem of cleaning up the empty cans that are sometimes left in the park.

    I urge you to consider this idea seriously. It is for the good of all.

closing —— Sincerely,

signature — Hester A. Martin

How to Write a Business Letter
1. Write the heading in the upper-right corner.
2. Write the inside address at the left margin.
3. Write the greeting under the inside address. Put a colon (:) after the greeting.
4. Write the body in paragraph form. Tell why you are writing to the person or business. Use a polite tone.
5. Write the closing in line with the heading. In a business letter, the closing is *Yours truly* or *Sincerely.*
6. Write your signature under the closing. Sign your full name. Then, print your name.

Business Letter, page 2

DIRECTIONS ➤ Read the example business letter on page 99. Then, answer the questions.

1. What is the topic of this letter? _____

_____

2. Is the writer for or against the topic?

_____

3. What are two reasons the writer gives to support this opinion?

_____

_____

4. How would you describe the closing of the letter?

_____

DIRECTIONS ➤ Think about a business letter that you would like to write. You can write to ask for information about a product, to complain about a product or service, or to praise a product or service. Fill in the chart below. Use the graphic organizer to plan your business letter.

To whom am I writing?	
What is my purpose?	
What tone should I use?	
What facts do I want to include?	

Business Letter, page 3

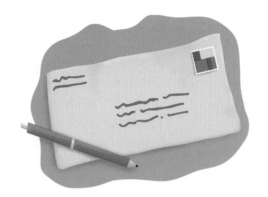

Tips for Writing a Business Letter
- Think of someone to write to.
- Think of something to write about. Will you complain or compliment?
- Write your business letter.
- Be polite but firm.
- Be sure to include all the parts.
- Fill out the envelope correctly.

heading _____

_____

_____

_____ inside address

_____

_____

_____

_____ greeting

body _____

_____

_____

_____

_____

_____

_____

_____

closing _____

signature _____

How-to Paragraph

A **how-to paragraph** gives directions or explains how to do something. Detail sentences in a how-to paragraph use time-order words to show the correct order of the steps.

Example:

Popping Popcorn in a Microwave Oven

Before you begin, be sure that you have popcorn that is especially packaged for microwave popping. Of course, you will need a microwave oven. Remove the plastic overwrap from the bag, and place it in the center of the microwave. Be very careful not to puncture or open the special bag the popcorn is in. You should set the microwave for full or 100 percent power. Then, set the timer for five minutes, and push the button to start. Stop the microwave when popping time slows to two to three seconds between pops. Remove the hot bag from the oven. You should shake the bag before opening it to increase flavor and to distribute the salt.

How to Write a How-to Paragraph

1. Write a topic sentence that names the process you are describing.
2. Add a detail sentence that tells what materials are needed.
3. Write detail sentences that tell the steps in the order they need to be done.
4. Use time-order words such as *first, next, then,* and *finally* to show the order of the steps.

How-to Paragraph, page 2

DIRECTIONS > Read the example how-to paragraph on page 102. Then, answer the questions.

1. What does this paragraph tell you how to do?

_____

2. How many items are listed as materials, and what are they?

_____

3. What is the first thing you must do?

_____

4. What is the next thing you do?

_____

5. What happens next?

_____

6. What do you do last?

_____

DIRECTIONS > Think about something you want to tell others how to do. Use this writing plan to help you.

WRITING PLAN

1. What will you tell others how to do?

2. What materials are needed?

3. What steps must the reader follow? Number the steps.

4. What time-order words will you use?

Tips for Writing a How-to Paragraph
• Choose one thing to teach someone.
• Think of all the materials that are needed.
• Think of all the steps someone should follow.
• Be sure to write about the steps in the order they must be done.
• Use time-order words to help the reader follow the steps.
• Tell the reader any additional tips that will make the process easier to do.

DIRECTIONS > Think about something you want to tell others how to do. Use your writing plan as a guide for writing your how-to paragraph.

_____

_____

_____

_____

_____

_____

_____

_____

_____

_____

_____

_____

_____

_____

_____

Information Paragraph

An **information paragraph** gives facts about one topic.
It has a topic sentence that tells the main idea. Detail sentences give facts about the main idea.
Examples:

Food in Cans — **title**

The idea of storing food in tin cans was developed in — **topic sentence**
England in 1810. A British merchant named Peter Durand is
responsible for this idea. It is interesting that no one invented
a can opener until fifty years later. British soldiers in 1812 tore — **detail sentences**
open canned rations with bayonets and pocket knives. They
were even known to shoot the cans open.

The Modern Can Opener — **title**

The can opener that we use today was invented — **topic sentence**
about 1870. It was invented by an American inventor
named William W. Lyman. It has a cutting wheel that rotates
around the can's edge. It was immediately popular, and it has
been changed only once. In 1925, a special wheel was added. — **detail sentences**
This was called the "feed wheel," and it made the can rotate
against the cutting wheel.

How to Write an Information Paragraph
1. Write a topic sentence that tells your main idea.
2. Write at least three detail sentences that give information about your main idea.
3. Think of a title for your information paragraph.

DIRECTIONS ▶ **Read the example information paragraphs on page 105. Then, answer the questions.**

1. What is the main idea of the first information paragraph?

_____

_____

2. What are two supporting details in the first information paragraph?

_____

_____

3. What is the topic sentence of the second information paragraph?

_____

_____

4. What are two supporting details in the second information paragraph?

_____

_____

DIRECTIONS ▶ **Think about an informative topic you would like to write about. Use this writing plan to help you.**

WRITING PLAN

Topic: _____

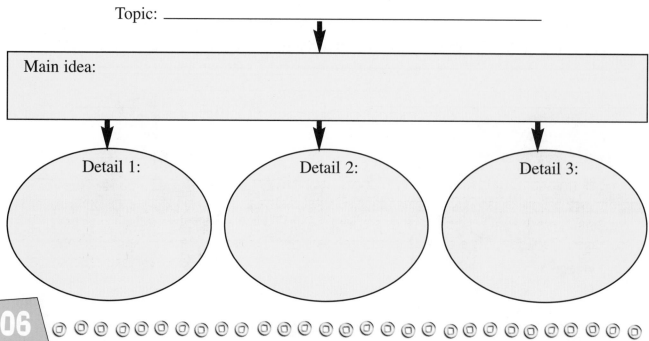

Main idea:

Detail 1:   Detail 2:   Detail 3:

Information Paragraph, page 3

Tips for Writing an Information Paragraph
- Choose one topic to write about.
- Write a title for your paragraph.
- Write a topic sentence that tells your main idea.
- Write at least three detail sentences that tell facts about the main idea.
- Be sure your facts are correct and complete.

DIRECTIONS ► Choose a topic you would like to write about. Use your writing plan as a guide for writing your information paragraph.

Compare and Contrast Paragraph

In a **compare and contrast paragraph**, a writer shows how two people, places, things, or ideas are alike or different. To compare means to show how two things are similar. To contrast means to show how two things are different.
Example:

> The Tasady tribe and the Ik tribe are two examples of people still living in the Stone Age. Neither tribe knew anything about the outside world until recently. The Tasady live in the mountain caves of the Philippine rain forests. The Ik live in the mountains of Uganda, and they build grass huts for shelter. There is plenty of food in the Philippine rain forests, so the Tasady are comfortable and fairly well off. The Ik, however, face a constant lack of food. Ik usually eat any food they find right away. The Tasady have a good chance of surviving; the Ik, on the other hand, face an uncertain future.

How to Write a Compare and Contrast Paragraph
1. Write a topic sentence that names the subjects and tells briefly how they are alike and different.
2. Give examples in the detail sentences that clearly tell how the subjects are alike and different.
3. Write about the likenesses or the differences in the same order you named them in the topic sentence.
4. Try to have at least three ways in which the subjects are alike or different.

Compare and Contrast Paragraph, page 2

DIRECTIONS ▷ **Read the example compare and contrast paragraph on page 108. Then, answer the questions.**

1. What is the topic sentence of the paragraph? _____

_____

2. What two subjects are being compared? _____

_____

3. What are three things that are similar about the two subjects?

_____

_____

4. What are three things that are different about the two subjects?

_____

_____

5. Does the last sentence of the paragraph compare or contrast the survival of the tribes?

_____

DIRECTIONS ▷ **Choose two things you want to write about. Then, use the Venn diagram to help you plan your writing. List what is true only about A in the A circle. List what is true only about B in the B circle. List what is true about both A and B where the circles overlap.**

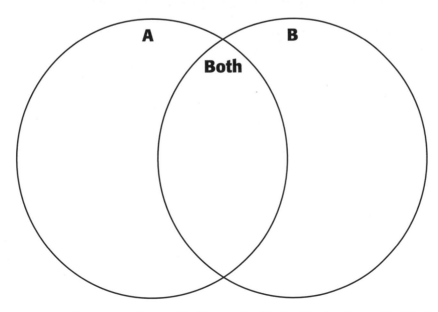

Tips for Writing a Compare and Contrast Paragraph
- Think about your two subjects.
- Decide how the two subjects are alike and different. Choose at least three important similarities and differences.
- Write a topic sentence that tells how the two subjects are alike and different.
- Explain how the two subjects are alike.
- Explain how the two subjects are different.
- Write about the likenesses or the differences in the same order you named them in the topic sentence.

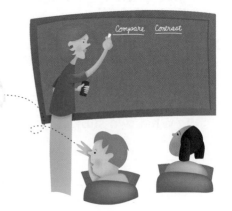

DIRECTIONS Choose two subjects you would like to compare and contrast. Use your Venn diagram to write your compare and contrast paragraph.

Cause and Effect Paragraph

A cause is an event that makes something else happen. An effect is something that happens as a result of a cause. One cause may have several effects. One effect may have several causes.

In a **cause and effect paragraph**, a writer focuses on a cause that results in certain effects or an effect that can be traced back to its causes. This type of paragraph can begin with either the cause or the effect.

Example:

> In the story "The Tournament," a girl named Katharine goes back in time. If Merlin had not reversed Katharine's wish in the story, history would have been very different. First of all, Katharine would have been the champion of the jousting tournament instead of Sir Lancelot. As a result, Sir Lancelot would have been dismissed from the Queen's order of knights. Furthermore, King Arthur's Round Table would have been dissolved and never heard of again.

How to Write a Cause and Effect Paragraph
1. Begin paragraphs of effect with a cause. Write a topic sentence that tells what happened. The detail sentences should all discuss effects.
2. Begin paragraphs of cause with an effect. Write a topic sentence that tells a result. The detail sentences should all discuss causes.
3. Write detail sentences in the order in which the effects or the causes happened.

 **DIRECTIONS** ▶ Read the example cause and effect paragraph on page 111. Then, answer the questions.

1. What caused history to be in danger of change?

_____

_____

2. What caused history not to be changed?

_____

_____

3. What would be three effects if history had been changed?

_____

_____

_____

_____

 **DIRECTIONS** ▶ Think of something that happened. What caused it to happen? What were the effects? Use the chart to organize your ideas.

WRITING PLAN

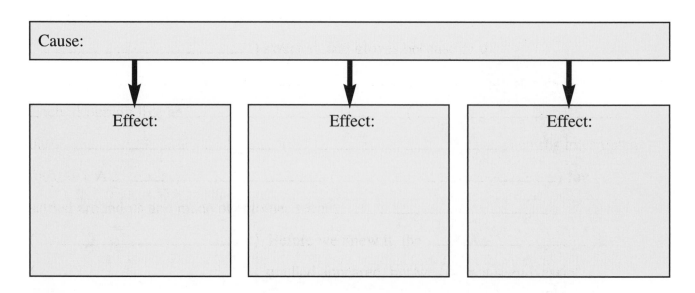

Tips for Writing a Cause and Effect Paragraph
- Think of something that happened.
- In your topic sentence, identify a cause or an effect.
- Clearly explain the cause that made something happen.
- Clearly explain the effect that happened because of something else.
- Try to include an end result or effect.

DIRECTIONS > Choose an event you would like to write about. Use your writing plan as a guide for writing your cause and effect paragraph.

_____

_____

_____

_____

_____

_____

_____

_____

_____

_____

_____

_____

_____

_____

_____

_____

_____

_____

Evaluation Paragraph

In an **evaluation paragraph**, a writer judges a subject or idea. Then, the writer provides reasons or examples to support this judgment. A writer might like or dislike something. A writer might also judge that something is good or bad.
Example:

> In the story "Two of Everything," Mr. and Mrs. Hak-Tak made doubles of themselves. They were very clever to make their doubles their neighbors. First, the Hak-Taks could not send their doubles away without telling the secret. Keeping them nearby was a clever way of protecting themselves. Second, building a house next door for their doubles gave Mr. and Mrs. Hak-Tak extra help around the farm. Most important, their doubles became Mr. and Mrs. Hak-Tak's best friends. This was the cleverest outcome of all.

How to Write an Evaluation Paragraph
1. In the topic sentence, state whom or what you will evaluate and your judgment about it.
2. Keep your audience in mind as you write.
3. Provide reasons or strong examples to support your judgment.
4. Write a concluding sentence that summarizes your judgment.

 **DIRECTIONS** > **Read the judgment and the three supporting reasons. Write *1* next to the most important reason, *2* next to the second most important reason, and *3* next to the least important reason.**

Athletic contests between schools are a bad idea.

_____ Such contests lead to bad feelings between schools, and sometimes violent behavior is the result.

_____ It is too expensive to transport students from one place to another.

_____ Athletes spend too much time practicing, and their schoolwork suffers.

Evaluation Paragraph, page 2

DIRECTIONS ▷ Read the example evaluation paragraph on page 114. Then, answer the questions.

1. What is being evaluated in the paragraph?

   _____

2. What judgment does the writer make about the Hak-Tak's creating doubles?

   _____

3. What is the least important example the writer gives to support the judgment?

   _____

   _____

4. What is the second most important example the writer gives to support the judgment?

   _____

   _____

5. What is the most important example the writer gives to support the judgment?

   _____

   _____

DIRECTIONS ▷ Think of a subject or an idea that you would like to evaluate. Then, use this writing plan to organize your evaluation paragraph.

WRITING PLAN

Topic Sentence: _____

_____

Example: _____

Example: _____

Example: _____

Tips for Writing an Evaluation Paragraph
• Choose one subject or idea to evaluate.
• Decide what your judgment will be.
• Identify your subject and your judgment in your topic sentence.
• Include at least three reasons or examples for your judgment.
• Put your least important reason first in your paragraph.
• Put your most important reason last in our paragraph.

DIRECTIONS Choose a subject or an idea you would like to evaluate. Use your writing plan as a guide for writing your evaluation paragraph.

_____

_____

_____

_____

_____

_____

_____

_____

_____

_____

_____

_____

_____

_____

_____

_____

Persuasive Paragraph

In a **persuasive paragraph**, a writer tries to make readers agree with his or her opinion on an issue.
Example:

Wisconsin should have a "Caddie Woodlawn Day" to celebrate the trust between Caddie and her Native American friends. This trust prevented a massacre and led to the peace between the two groups. "Caddie Woodlawn Day" would remind us to settle problems by peaceful means. In addition, this holiday would give us a reason to practice our ancestors' customs. Then, we would be reminded to appreciate their way of life. Because this holiday would help us to remember Caddie Woodlawn, the state legislature should vote in favor of this idea.

opinion in topic sentence

reasons and facts

strongest reason last

restated opinion or call for action

How to Write a Persuasive Paragraph

1. Write a topic sentence that states the issue and your opinion about it.
2. Keep in mind the audience that you want to convince.
2. Give at least three reasons that will convince your audience to agree with you. Include these reasons in the detail sentences.
3. Explain each reason with one or more examples.
4. Save your strongest reason for last.
5. At the end of your paragraph, tell your opinion again. Ask your reader to feel the same way.

Persuasive Paragraph, page 2

DIRECTIONS ▸ Read the example persuasive paragraph on page 117. Then, answer the questions.

1. What is the writer's main idea in this paragraph?

_____

_____

2. What are two reasons the writer gives to support the main idea?

_____

_____

_____

3. What call for action does the writer have in the last sentence?

_____

_____

DIRECTIONS ▸ Think of something you feel strongly about. Then, use this writing plan to organize your persuasive paragraph.

WRITING PLAN

My Opinion

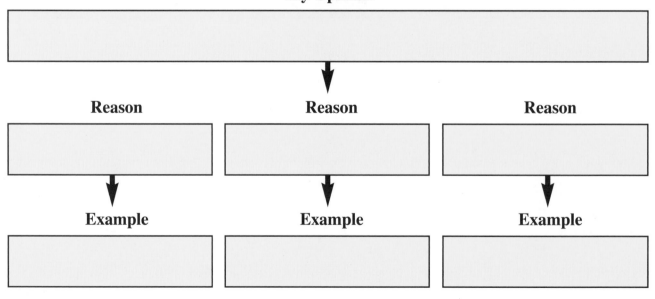

Tips for Writing a Persuasive Paragraph
• Choose a topic that you feel strongly about.
• State your opinion in your topic sentence.
• Write good reasons to support your opinion.
• Try to have at least three good reasons.
• Save your strongest reason for last.
• Try to give an example for each reason.
• At the end of your paragraph, restate your opinion. Tell the reader to take some action.

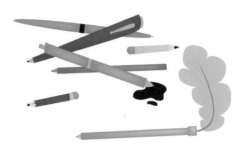

DIRECTIONS ➤ **Choose a topic that you have an opinion about. Use your writing plan as a guide for writing your persuasive paragraph.**

_____

_____

_____

_____

_____

_____

_____

_____

_____

_____

_____

_____

_____

_____

_____

_____

_____

Writing for a Test

Many tests have sections that require you to demonstrate your writing skills. You are usually given a topic and a time limit. The writing process can help you adapt your writing style to meet this challenge. Here are some tips for writing better on a test.

PREWRITING

Analyzing a Topic
• Do I understand the question?
• Am I being asked to compare, contrast, give an opinion, explain, or describe?
• What form of writing will be most effective?

Gathering Information
• Am I allowed to look in books while I write?
• Would it help to make a rough outline before I write?

DRAFTING

• Can I focus my writing by beginning with a clear topic sentence?
• How much time do I have for this assignment?

RESPONDING AND REVISING

• Have I answered the question completely?
• Should I add any additional information?
• Are there any incorrect statements that I should change?
• Have I checked the spelling of every word?
• Have I checked for mistakes in grammar?

FINAL DRAFT

• Do I have time to make a neater copy?
• If not, are there any sloppy sections I should write on another page?

TIMED WRITING

You have probably taken timed tests before. What are some ways to do well during a timed writing test? Follow these tips to make a timed test go more smoothly:

- Stay calm. Don't panic. Take a deep breath and relax.
- For a writing test, remember to check your task and your purpose. (Unless you are told otherwise, your audience is the person who will read the test.)
- Plan how you will use your time. If this is a writing test, decide how much time you need to spend prewriting, drafting, revising, proofreading, and writing the final draft.
- Use your time wisely once you start writing.
- If you begin to run out of time, decide if you can combine some steps. Your goal is to finish.

WRITTEN PROMPTS

 A written prompt is a statement or a question that asks you to complete a writing task.

- A narrative prompt asks you to tell a story.
- A persuasive prompt asks you to convince the reader.
- An expository prompt asks you to inform or explain.
- A descriptive prompt asks you to describe something.
- An evaluative prompt asks you to judge something.
- A comparison-contrast prompt asks you to discuss the similarities and the differences between two things.

PICTURE PROMPTS

A picture prompt is a statement or question about a picture. It asks you to tell something about the picture. The prompt also tells the purpose for writing. Study the picture carefully before you begin writing.

Using a Dictionary

The order of letters from *A* to *Z* is called **alphabetical order**. Words in a dictionary are listed in alphabetical order.

There are two **guide words** at the top of every dictionary page. The word on the left is the first word on the page. The word on the right is the last word. All the other words on the page are in alphabetical order between the guide words.

Each word that is defined in the dictionary is an **entry word**. An entry word usually appears in dark print. Each entry word appears in alphabetical order and is divided into syllables.

An **entry** is all the information about an entry word.

A **definition** is the meaning of a word. Many words have more than one definition. Each definition is numbered.

The **part of speech** tells whether a word is a noun, a verb, or some other part of speech. The parts of speech in a dictionary entry usually are abbreviated this way.

noun—n.   verb—v.   adjective—adj.   adverb—adv.   pronoun—pron.

A definition is often followed by an **example** that shows how to use the word.

float [flōt] **1** *v.* To rest or cause to rest on the surface of a liquid, such as water, without sinking: A life preserver *floats*. **2** *n.* An object that floats or holds up something else in a liquid, as an anchored raft at a beach or a piece of cork attached to a fishing line. **3** *v.* To be carried along gently on the surface of a liquid or through the air; drift: Fog *floated* over the city. **4** *v.* To move lightly and without effort: The skater *floated* across the ice. **5** *n.* A wheeled platform or truck on which an exhibit is carried in a parade.

DIRECTIONS ➤ **Use the example entry to answer the following questions.**

1. How many definitions are given for *float*? _____

2. Which part of speech is the first definition of *float*? _____

3. As what other part of speech can *float* be used? _____

4. Which definition tells the meaning of *float* in the following sentences?

The balloon <u>floated</u> up to the ceiling. _____

Have you ever ridden a <u>float</u> in a parade? _____

Using a Dictionary, page 2

A **syllable** is a word part that has only one vowel sound. Each entry word in the dictionary is divided into syllables.

A **pronunciation** follows each entry word. Letters and symbols show how the word is pronounced. It also shows the number of syllables in the word.

Example:

il • lu • sion [i • lo͞o′ zhen] *n.* **1** A false, mistaken idea or belief: to lose childish *illusions*. **2** A deceiving appearance or the false impression it gives: an optical *illusion*.

In a word with two or more syllables, the **accent mark** (′) in the pronunciation shows which syllable is said with the most force.

A **pronunciation key** explaining the pronunciation marks usually appears at the beginning of a dictionary. A brief key like the one below is often found at the bottom of dictionary pages.

a	add	i	it	o͝o	took	oi	oil
ā	ace	ī	ice	o͞o	pool	ou	pout
â	care	o	odd	u	up	ng	ring
ä	palm	ō	open	û	burn	th	thin
e	end	ô	order	yo͞o	fuse	th	this
ē	equal					zh	vision

ə = { a in *above*   e in *sicken*   i in *possible*
      { o in *melon*   u in *circus*

DIRECTIONS ➤ **Write the word shown in each dictionary respelling. Then, use each word in a sentence. Use the dictionary if you need help with pronunciations or definitions.**

1. [op′ ti • kəl] _____

_____

2. [ri • flek′ shən] _____

_____

3. [mə • jish′ ən] _____

_____

4. [nā′ chər] _____

_____

Using a Thesaurus

A **thesaurus** is a book that lists synonyms, words that have nearly the same meaning, and antonyms, words that mean the opposite of a word. Many thesauruses are like dictionaries. The entry words are listed in dark print in alphabetical order. Guide words at the top of the page tell which words can be found on the page. Good writers use a thesaurus to find vivid and exact words to make their writing more interesting.

DIRECTIONS ▸ Replace each underlined word or words with words that express the meaning in a more exact and vivid way. You may want to refer to a thesaurus.

1. When Harvey was growing up, his family was <u>very large</u>. _____

2. At one time Harvey counted <u>about</u> sixty cousins. _____

3. They all lived on a large farm, <u>taking care of</u> animals and crops. _____

4. Everyone <u>worked hard</u>. _____

5. In the 1930s, the family lost the land they had <u>worked</u> for so long. _____

6. Things became very <u>hard</u> for the family. _____

7. Harvey's parents found jobs in the <u>shops</u> in town. _____

8. Harvey, an <u>ambitious</u> young man, decided that he would have his own store someday.

_____

9. Thirty years later, Harvey owned one of the largest chains of stores in the <u>country</u>.

_____

DIRECTIONS ▸ Write sentences using exact, vivid synonyms of the words in parentheses.

10. (small) _____

_____

11. (house) _____

_____

12. (walk) _____

_____

Using an Encyclopedia

An **encyclopedia** is a set of books that contains information on many subjects. The articles are arranged in alphabetical order in different books, called volumes. Guide words at the top of the page show the first subject on the page. Looking up some subjects may be difficult, though. The names of people and some cities may have two words. How do you know which word to use to find information in an encyclopedia?

How To Use an Encyclopedia
1. Always look up the last name of a person.
   Example: To find an article on Babe Ruth, look under *Ruth.*
2. Always look up the first name of a city, state, or country.
   Example: To find an article on New York City, look under *New.*
3. Always look up the most important word in the name of a general topic.
   Example: To find an article on the brown bear, look under *bear.*

DIRECTIONS ⟩ Write the word you would look under to find an article on each of these subjects.

1. Susan B. Anthony _____

2. salt water _____

3. New Mexico _____

4. lakes in Scotland _____

5. Rio de Janeiro _____

6. United Kingdom _____

7. modern literature _____

8. breeds of horses _____

9. Gila monster _____

10. Robert Frost _____

11. Industrial Revolution _____

12. Queen Victoria _____

Using an Encyclopedia, page 2

Remember that an encyclopedia is a set of books that contains information on many subjects. Each book in an encyclopedia is called a **volume**. The volumes are arranged in alphabetical order. Each article in an encyclopedia is called an **entry**. Each volume is labeled on its spine with the beginning letter or letters of its first and last entries.

Many encyclopedias have a separate **index**. The index is usually the last volume in the encyclopedia. The index lists all the entries in alphabetical order. Next to the entry are the volume and page numbers.

Underground Railroad
  United States History **U 275** *with map*
    See also Slavery *in this index.*
  Abolitionists **A 87**
  Civil War (Origins) **C 160**
  Tubman, Harriet **T 232**
    See also the list of Related Readings in the Black Americans *article.*

> **DIRECTIONS**   Use the encyclopedia index above to answer the following questions.

1. In how many volumes might you find information on the Underground Railroad?

2. To what volume and page would you turn to find an article on Harriet Tubman?

3. Which entry also contains a map?

4. Which entry refers the reader to another entry in the index?

5. In what section of the Civil War entry would you find information on the Underground Railroad?

6. Under what entry might you find related readings about Harriet Tubman?

Using the Internet

The computer is a powerful research tool. The **Internet**, a system using telephone and cable lines to send signals, helps you to find almost any information in the blink of an eye. You can communicate instantly with other people by sending electronic mail. Some computers let you see the people as you talk. The key to using the computer as a research tool is knowing what keywords to use to start the Internet search. It takes some practice, but you never know what interesting place you can visit or what information you can find. Here are some hints to speed up the search.

How to Use the Internet
1. Make a list of keywords or names.
2. Choose a search engine that has a directory to narrow the topic.
3. Type in two or three keywords.
4. Type in different combinations of keywords until the topic titles focus on the information you need.

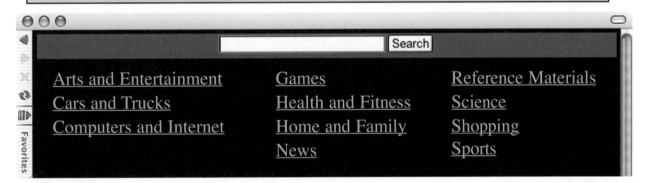

DIRECTIONS ▷ **Use the example Internet directory to choose the category you would search for these subjects.**

1. bicycle champion Lance Armstrong _____

2. how to multiply fractions _____

3. the events at a local museum _____

4. buying a new pair of shoes _____

5. download a new game _____

6. author Shel Silverstein _____

7. astronaut Sally Ride _____

8. which Native American groups lived in your area _____

Parts of a Book

The **title page** tells the name of a book and the name of the author. It also gives the name of the publisher and the city of publication.

The **copyright page** tells when the book was published. It sometimes lists the titles of other books from which material was reprinted by permission. This is the acknowledgments section.

The **table of contents** comes after the title page. It lists each unit, chapter, story, or section in the order in which it appears in the book. A table of contents usually lists the page on which each part of the book begins.

Many nonfiction books also have an **index**. An index is an alphabetical list of all the topics in a book. Indexes include the page or pages on which each topic appears.

Giants **In Myth and Legend** by Gloria Kim KING PRESS, INC. New York Chicago	Copyright © 1983 by King Press, Inc. **Acknowledgments** Ace Publishing Company: from *Giants* by Val Meyer. Copyright © 1981 by Val Meyer. All rights reserved. Printed in the United States of America.	**CONTENTS** The Greek Titans.....................1 The Greek Cyclopes ....17 Jack and the Beanstalk..........21 Jack the Giant-Killer.............35 The Iroquois Stone Giants .....45 Paul Bunyan.........................51 Glossary ....65 Index 73
title page	copyright page	table of contents

DIRECTIONS ▷ Use the example pages to answer the following questions.

1. What is the title of this book? _____

2. Which company published the book? _____

3. When and where was the book printed? _____

4. How many chapters are there? _____

5. How many chapters tell of giants that are Greek? _____

6. On what page could you begin to read about Paul Bunyan? _____

7. On what page does the index begin? _____

8. Which is the first page on which you might read about Polyphemus, one of the Cyclopes?

_____

Reading for Information

Skimming is a quick reading method. To skim is to look at material in order to note its general subject, its divisions, and its major headings.

Scanning is also a quick reading method. To scan is to look quickly at a particular passage, searching for key words.

DIRECTIONS ▷ Skim the table of contents of this book to answer questions 1–3. Scan the page from the book to answer questions 4–6.

Bring in all objects that are usually left outside, such as lawn furniture or garbage cans. If you cannot bring them inside, tie them down securely. Board up your windows so that they will not be broken by objects carried by the wind. When the hurricane hits, stay inside and listen to your radio for information. Do not go outside until the authorities announce that it is safe.

1. How many general subjects will this book cover? _____

   What are they? _____

2. What does Chapter 1 of each part explain? _____

3. What do Chapters 2 and 3 of each part explain? _____

   _____

4. What should you do with lawn furniture if you cannot bring it inside?

   _____

5. Why should you board up your windows? _____

   _____

6. When can you go outside again? _____

   _____

Taking Notes

Good writers take notes to remember the facts they find when doing research for a report.

It is often helpful to write notes on cards. When preparing to write a report, the writer can put the cards in order according to the topic.

Example:

> The Mythological Zoo by Elizabeth Dixon, pages 20–29
> Which Greek and Roman gods had "pet" birds?
>   Zeus: eagle
>   Hera: peacock
>   Apollo: crow

How to Take Notes

1. Record the name of the book or magazine from which you are taking the information.
2. List the main topic of the material.
3. Write the most important facts and details.
4. Use key words and phrases. You need not write complete sentences.
5. Be sure your notes are accurate and readable.

 **DIRECTIONS** ➤ **Read this information taken from page 21 of The Mythological Zoo. Write notes that answer the question, "What are the symbols of Zeus?"**

     The Greeks and the Romans both had many gods. However, each of these ancient peoples had one god whom they considered to be the most important. Jupiter was considered the king of the Roman gods. Zeus held the same position for the Greeks. Jupiter's symbols were the king's scepter and the thunderbolt. Zeus was known by these two symbols, as well as by the oak tree and the eagle.

_____

_____

_____

_____

_____

Taking Notes, page 2

When taking notes, remember to write down the name of your source. You should also write down the most important information in the source. Take notes only on the material you will use in your essay or report.

DIRECTIONS → **Read the following paragraph. As you read, take notes on the lines below. Remember to focus on key points and to use abbreviations.**

One of the hottest and driest places in North America is Death Valley, in California. An average of only about one and one half inches of rain falls each year in Death Valley, and in some years it does not rain at all. The valley is the bottom of a lake that dried up in prehistoric times, leaving clay and salt in the center of the valley and sand dunes to the north. Near Badwater is the lowest spot in North America. It is 282 feet below sea level!

My Notes: _____

_____

_____

_____

_____

DIRECTIONS → **Now read over the notes you took. Use your notes to answer the questions.**

1. How did you choose the points to include in your notes?

_____

2. What abbreviations did you use in your notes?

_____

3. Why is it important to take good notes?

_____

Summary

A **summary** is a short sentence or paragraph that tells the main idea and the details in a story or selection. To summarize any writing, you must pay attention to the details. Using the question words *who, what, where, when,* and *why* can help you find the important details to include in a summary. There are some things you leave out of a summary. That is because they are less important than the main idea and the details. They may make the story more interesting, but you can summarize the story or selection without them. A summary table can help you organize the information to write a summary.

DIRECTIONS ➤ **Read the paragraph. Then, complete the summary table.**

Florida is a popular state for tourists. Millions of Americans from colder climates visit there every year. These visitors, often called "snowbirds" by people who live year-round in Florida, show up when snow is on the ground in the northern part of the United States. The northerners think that Florida's beautiful beaches and tourist attractions make it the best place to visit in the winter.

Who:	Summary:
What:	
Where:	
When:	
Why:	

Paraphrasing

Paraphrasing means to restate an idea in your own words. For example, you read a paragraph by another writer. How would you tell the information in the paragraph? You should not copy what the other writer has written. Instead, you would tell the information in your own words. When you do, you paraphrase what the other writer has written.

Example:

Writer's words: Maureen could hardly believe she was going to be in fifth grade this year. She was very excited. But she was nervous, too. The fifth grade was in a different school. The students in her class would be the youngest students in the school. She wondered if the older students would make fun of the younger ones. At the same time, Maureen thought it would be fun to be in a new school with older students. Her stomach was full of butterflies!

Your paraphrased version: Maureen had mixed feelings about going into the fifth grade.

DIRECTIONS → Read each paragraph. Then write, in your own words, a sentence or two to tell what the paragraph is about.

Greg was furious. A group of boys had invited Greg to go to the movies with them, but Greg's mother had said that he couldn't go. She did not like the idea of boys his age going to a movie without an adult. Greg sat in his room all night and thought about how angry he was at his mother. He also thought about how embarrassed he would feel when he saw his friends again.

1. In your own words, what is this paragraph about?

_____

_____

The next day, Greg found out that the boys who had gone to the movie had not had a very good time. One of them had begun a popcorn fight in the theater. People had complained, and the boys had to leave the movie. They had all gotten into trouble with their parents. Greg couldn't help feeling glad that he had not gone after all.

2. In your own words, what is this paragraph about?

_____

_____

Using Quotations

Good writers use **quotations** from oral and written sources. Quotations are the exact words that are in a book or that a speaker says. Quotations are enclosed in quotation marks (" ").

DIRECTIONS ▷ Each numbered sentence below is the topic sentence of a paragraph in a research report about whales. The box contains sentences with quotations that might be used in the report. Before each topic sentence, write the letter of the quotation sentence that should be included in that paragraph.

---

a. "These magnificent creatures are even larger than the famous dinosaurs that died out so long ago," commented Dr. Romley.

b. Said Dr. Schultz, "Although international laws ban hunting, some species of whales are still in danger of extinction."

c. Mr. Walters explained, "The whale's nostrils, located on top of its head, can be tightly closed so that no water leaks in."

d. "I am still thrilled every time I hear these whales 'talking' to each other," said Mr. Clark.

e. "Though we often think of whales as huge animals," said Ms. Kwong, "some species are barely four feet long."

f. "A baleen whale has no teeth. Instead, it has thin plates, called baleen, in its mouth," added Mr. Walters.

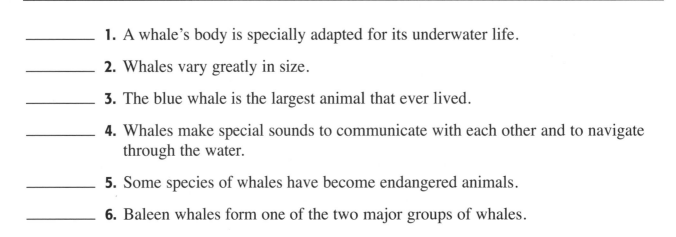

_____ **1.** A whale's body is specially adapted for its underwater life.

_____ **2.** Whales vary greatly in size.

_____ **3.** The blue whale is the largest animal that ever lived.

_____ **4.** Whales make special sounds to communicate with each other and to navigate through the water.

_____ **5.** Some species of whales have become endangered animals.

_____ **6.** Baleen whales form one of the two major groups of whales.

Outline

A writer uses an **outline** to organize the information he or she has gathered for a research report.
Example:

Bird Myths and Mysteries
I. Birds in Myth and Legend
    A. Birds of the Greek gods
    B. Birdlike monsters

II. Birds as Modern Symbols
    A. Of people's characteristics
    B. Of political points of view

How to Write an Outline
1. Write a title that tells the subject of your report. Capitalize each important word in the title.
2. Write the main topics. Use a Roman numeral and a period before each topic.
3. Capitalize each important word in a main topic.
4. Write subtopics under each main topic. Use a capital letter followed by a period for each subtopic. Begin each subtopic with a capital letter.
5. Do not write a *I* without a *II* or an *A* without a *B*.
6. Plan one paragraph for each main topic in your outline.

 **DIRECTIONS**   Read each line of the outline. If the line is correct, write *correct.* If not, rewrite the line correctly.

the job of a Mother bird   _____

  I. Find a good place for a nest   _____
    A. Dry enough   _____
    b. warm enough   _____
    c out of reach of cats   _____

 II. make the nest   _____
    a big enough   _____
    B. Snug enough   _____
    c. sides tall enough   _____
    d. inside Soft enough   _____

III. Take care of eggs   _____
    a. Sit on them   _____
    b. keep them warm   _____

Outline, page 2

In an outline, remember to use a Roman numeral and a period before each main topic. Indent each subtopic. Use a capital letter and a period before each subtopic. Capitalize the first word in each topic and subtopic. Capitalize each important word in the outline's title.

DIRECTIONS ▸ **Read the following paragraphs. Then, complete the outline below.**

The smallest living parts of your body are cells. Although they are the building blocks of your body, you cannot see them unless you use a microscope. There are many different kinds of cells, such as bone cells and skin cells.

Tissues are groups of cells working together. Just as there are different kinds of cells, there are different kinds of tissues. Two kinds are fat tissue and muscle tissue. Each kind has a different function in your body.

When groups of tissues work together, organs are formed. Each organ does a different job; however, all of your organs need to work together for your body to operate successfully.

I. Cells

   A. _____

   B. _____

   C. _____

      1. _____

      2. _____

II. _____

   A. _____

   B. _____

      1. _____

      2. _____

   C. _____

III. _____

   A. _____

   B. _____

   C. _____

Rough Draft

A writer quickly puts all of his or her ideas on paper in a **rough draft**.

How to Write a Rough Draft
1. Read your outline and notes. Keep them near you as you write.
2. Follow your outline to write a rough draft. Do not add anything that is not on your outline. Do not leave out anything.
3. Write one paragraph for each Roman numeral in your outline.
4. Write freely. Do not worry about mistakes now. You will revise later.
5. Read over your rough draft. Make notes on changes you want to make.

 DIRECTIONS Choose one of the partial outlines below. Then, write a topic sentence and two detail sentences based upon the points in the outline.

1. I. Dodo Bird Is Extinct
   A. Could not fly
   B. Had short, stubby legs

2. I. Family Life of Birds
   A. Selecting a territory
   B. Building a nest

3. I. Bird Migration
   A. Why birds migrate
   B. Where birds migrate

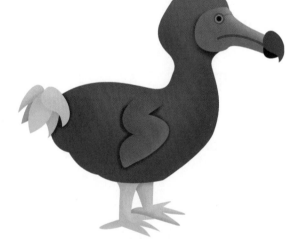

Topic sentence: _____

_____

Detail sentence 1: _____

_____

Detail sentence 2: _____

_____

Bibliography

A **bibliography** lists all the information a writer uses in a research report. The bibliography gives credit to the authors of the information used. A bibliography is also known as a "works cited" list.

How to Write a Bibliography

1. List the sources in alphabetical order by the author's last name or by the title if there is no author given.
2. After the author's name, write the title of the book or magazine source. Then, write the name of the publisher and the date of publication.
3. An Internet resource lists two dates. The first date tells the day the article was published. The second date is the day you found the article online.

Magazine Article
Bonfield, J. E. "Bird Clothes." Owl, November 1986: 26–29.

Book
Dixon, Elizabeth. The Mythological Zoo. New York: Bendix Books, 1986.

Encyclopedia
"Owls." Collier's Encyclopedia. Vol. 18. 1999 edition.

Internet
Smith, Donald. "On Silent Wings." May 2001. Online. 24 March 2005
        <www.owltime.net>.

DIRECTIONS ▷ **Use the model bibliography to answer these questions.**

1. Who wrote The Mythological Zoo? _____

2. In which volume of the encyclopedia was "Owls" found? _____

3. In which magazine issue does "Bird Clothes" appear? _____

4. At which Internet site can "On Silent Wings" be found? _____

5. When was the article "On Silent Wings" found online by the student?

_____

Analyzing a Research Report

A **research report** gives information about a topic. It draws facts from various sources. It has a title, an introduction, a body, and a conclusion.

DIRECTIONS ▶ Read the research report. Answer the questions that follow.

Many of our superstitions came to us from very ancient sources. The idea that one should knock on wood for good luck, for example, is a 4,000-year-old custom that began with some Native American tribes of North America. Noticing that the oak was struck often by lightning, members of the tribe thought that it must be the dwelling place of a sky god. They also thought that boasting of a future personal deed was bad luck and meant the thing would never happen. Knocking on an oak tree was a way of contacting the sky god and being forgiven for boasting.

Another interesting superstition is that it is bad luck to open an umbrella indoors. In eighteenth-century England, umbrellas had stiff springs and very strong metal spokes. Opening one indoors could indeed cause an accident. It could injure someone or break a fragile object. This superstition came about for practical reasons.

1. What would be a good title for this research report?

_____

2. What is the topic of the first paragraph?

_____

3. What is the topic of the second paragraph?

_____

4. What are three details from the first paragraph?

_____

_____

_____

_____

Research Report

After making the changes to the rough draft, the writer can complete the final copy of the research report.

Example:

Bird Myths and Mysteries

Birds have always been part of myths and legends. In ancient Greece, many birds were special to the gods. The eagle was a symbol of Zeus. The peacock symbolized Hera, and the crow stood for Apollo. Stories tell of birdlike monsters called Harpies and of a huge, terrible bird called a roe.

Birds are still used as symbols today. Many expressions compare people to birds. A person may be "wise as an owl" or "proud as a peacock." Names of birds can also be found in the world of politics. Senators are often described as hawks or doves, depending on their political point of view.

Scientists have solved some of the mysteries about birds, but many others remain. How do the ptarmigan's feathers act as a camouflage? Why does the arctic tern migrate from the Arctic to the Antarctic? These and other mysteries are sure to keep people fascinated by birds.

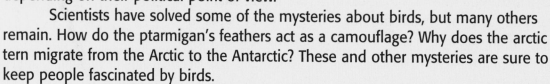

How to Write a Research Report
1. Read over your rough draft. Add any material you might have forgotten.
2. Make all revising and editing changes.
3. Write the title of your report.
4. Write the report from your rough draft and your notes.
5. Indent the first sentence of each paragraph.
6. Complete your bibliography.

DIRECTIONS ▸ **Read the example research report on this page. Then, choose a topic that interests you, and write your own report. Remember to take notes, make an outline, write a rough draft, complete a bibliography, and then write your report. Save all your notes to turn in with your report. Your report should be at least three paragraphs long and should have a title.**

Answer Key

Unit 1

Page 6
Descriptions of what the nouns name may vary.
1. sense, thing; smell, thing; nose, thing;
2. people, person; smell, thing; food, thing;
grass, thing; rain, thing; **3.** People, person; lot,
thing; enjoyment, thing; odors, thing; **4.** eggs,
thing; odor, thing; **5.** sense, thing; smell, thing;
person, person; danger, thing; **6.–7.** Sentences
will vary.

Page 7
1. common: scientist; proper: Maryland,
2. common: friends; proper: Benjamin Banneker,
3. common: People, accomplishments; proper:
United States, **4.** proper: Banneker, Washington,
D.C., **5.** common: man, memory, **6.** common:
astronomer, nights, stars, planets, **7.** common:
scientists, planets; proper: Mars, Jupiter,
8. common: changes, country; proper: Banneker,
1.–8. Rewritten sentences will vary.

Page 8
1. tornado, singular; hurricane, singular;
2. minutes, plural; hours, plural; **3.** winds, plural;
4. air, singular; fire, singular; **5.** conditions, plural;
signs, plural; **6.** The girls ate their lunches on the
school benches., **7.** The young ladies looked at the
dark clouds overhead., **8.** Strong winds picked up
boxes of books by the library doors.

Page 9
1. trout, **2.** fish or fishes, **3.** heroes, **4.** women,
5. men, **6.** mice, **7.** beliefs, **8.** wolves, **9.** oxen,
10. calves, **11.** children, **12.** feet, **13.** lives

Page 10
1. My friend's mother had a baby yesterday.,
2. The baby's teeth are not in yet., **3.** The child's
head is still soft., **4.** The bib's tie is torn., **5.** The
crib's sheets are pink., **6.** The uncle's smile is
happy., **7.** The grandmother's gift is a new
blanket., **8.** The father's pleasure is easy to see.,
9. The infant's eyes are blue., **10.** My friend's life
will be different now.

Page 11
1. Imagine the children's surprise!., **2.** They found
the robins' baby on the sidewalk., **3.** They returned
it to the parents' nest., **4.** They watched the adult
birds' activities for a while., **5.** The birds' fear was
apparent., **6.** The humans' odor was on the baby
bird., **7.** The bird was now the young people's
responsibility., **8.** The students' job was to find a
shoe box., **9.** The parents' job was to find some
soft lining.

Page 12
1. They, Explorers; **2.** It, animal; **3.** them, animals
or kangaroos; **4.** They, birds; **5.** It, platypus;
6. They, Scientists; **7.** It, coolabah or tree;
8. It, flower or kangaroo paw

Page 13
1. We read about the Wrights last week., **2.** It
was he who found the book., **3.** They grew up in
Dayton, Ohio., **4.** He was a bishop there., **5.** She
helped care for them., **6.** It was a gift from their
father., **7.** He was four years older than Orville.,
8. On December 17, 1903, it took place., **9.** It
lasted 12 seconds., **10.** They were 13 seconds,
15 seconds, and 59 seconds.

Page 14
1. Darkness covered them., **2.** The game wardens
noticed it., **3.** Then, the game wardens saw
them., **4.** Two men and a woman were searching
it for alligators., **5.** The game wardens pushed it
out of the brush., **6.** The wardens raced toward
them., **7.** The powerful engine moved it quickly
over the water., **8.** The poachers quickly dumped
them back into the water., **9.** The wardens
searched the inside of it.

Page 15
1. He, subject pronoun; **2.** him, object pronoun;
3. We, subject pronoun; **4.** them, object pronoun;
5. She, subject pronoun; **6.** her, object pronoun;
7. They, subject pronoun; **8.** them, object
pronoun; **9.** She, subject pronoun; **10.** them,
object pronoun

Page 16
1. myself, **2.** himself, **3.** itself, **4.** herself,
5. yourselves, **6.** ourselves, **7.** yourself,
8. ourselves, **9.** herself, **10.** myself, **11.** herself,
12. himself

Page 17
1. their, before a noun; **2.** Its, before a noun;
3. hers, stands alone; **4.** Her, before a noun;
5. theirs, stands alone; **6.** our, before a noun;
7. her; **8.** hers; **9.** their; **10.** your

Page 18
1. He, Mr. Les Harsten; **2.** them, plants; **3.** He,
Les; **4.** It, sound; **5.** it, plant; **6.** them, sounds;
7. It, recording; **8.** They, plants; **9.** It, music;
10. They, plants

Page 19
1. spectacular, what kind; **2.** superb, what kind;
beautiful, what kind; **3.** winter, what kind;
4. many, how many; different, what kind; **5.** red,
what kind; pink, what kind; violet, what kind;
white, what kind; **6.** spongy, what kind; acid,
what kind; **7.** three, how many; four, how many;
flowering, what kind; **8.** bright, what kind;
colorful, what kind; special, what kind

Page 20
1. Greek, Greece; **2.** Spartan, Sparta; **3.** Athenian,
Athens; **4.** Roman, Rome; **5.** Korean, Korea;
6. Romanian, Romania; **7.** English;
8. Norwegian; **9.** Canadian; **10.** American

Page 21
1. crunchy, peanuts; **2.** salty, They; **3.** red, skin;
4. delicious, seeds; **5.** inedible, seeds; **6.** popular,
They; **7.** healthful, snacks; **8.** sour, apples;
9. crisp and juicy, fruit; **10.** noisy, vegetable;
11.–15. Adjectives will vary.

Page 22
1. a, **2.** These, **3.** the, **4.** this, **5.** a, **6.** the, **7.** a,
8. this, **9.** these, **10.** those

Page 23
1. more wonderful, **2.** most beautiful, **3.** highest,
4. deeper, **5.** biggest, **6.** largest, **7.** easiest, **8.** most
unusual, **9.** stranger, **10.** more excited, **11.** most
interesting, **12.** oldest

Page 24
1. better, **2.** less, **3.** worst, **4.** more, **5.** worse,
6. more, **7.** Many, **8.** most

Page 25
1. linking: felt, **2.** action: left, **3.** action: needed,
4. action: looked, **5.** action: saw, **6.** action: ran;
studied, **7.** linking: appeared, **8.** action: pulled;
action: moved, **9.** action: slid, **10.** action: hurried,
11. action: bowed, **12.** linking: was

Page 26
1. told, main verb; **2.** looking, main verb; **3.** tell,
main verb; **4.** was, helping verb; **5.** leaned, main
verb; **6.** was, helping verb; **7.** fallen, main verb;
8. was, helping verb

Page 27
1. likes, **2.** visits, **3.** comes, **4.** fix, **5.** mixes,
6. takes, **7.** show, **8.** wishes, **9.** worries,
10. watches, **11.** makes, **12.** needs

Page 28
1. walked, **2.** sampled, **3.** seemed, **4.** described,
5. served, **6.** sipped, **7.** fried, **8.** tried, **9.** passed,
10. pinned, **11.** featured, **12.** tasted

Page 29
1. will happen, **2.** will hunt, **3.** will gather, **4.**
Will Sam miss, **5.** Will they search, **6.** will not
find, **7.** will remember, **8.** will cook, **9.** will float,
10. will hide, **11.** will notice, **12.** Will Sam leave

Page 30
1. look, present; **2.** have, present; **3.** climbs,
present; **4.** make, present; **5.** climbed, past;
6. jumps, present; **7.** will see, future; **8.** will go,
future; **9.** will ride, future; **10.** will tell, future;
11. Sam will see ten lizards.; **12.** I will see only
four.; **13.** Some lizards will change colors.

Page 31
1. done, **2.** rode, **3.** gave, **4.** ran, **5.** come, **6.** ate,
7. saw, **8.** said, **9.** took, **10.** thought, **11.** written,
12. went

Page 32
1. her, **2.** immigrants, **3.** torch, **4.** hope, freedom,
5. statue, **6.–16.** Sentences will vary. Be sure each
sentence contains an appropriate direct object.

Page 33
1. carefully, how; **2.** First, when; **3.** Next, when;
4. Then, when; **5.** Finally, when; **6.** firmly, how;
7. surely, how; **8.** joyfully, how; **9.** higher, where;
10. Soon, when; **11.** down, where;
12.–13. Sentences will vary. Be sure each
sentence contains an adverb.

Page 34
1. more eagerly, **2.** more strongly, **3.** most
courageously, **4.** more completely, **5.** more often,
6. most convincingly, **7.** better, **8.** worse,
9. better, **10.** well

Page 35
1. very, **2.** extremely, **3.** carefully, **4.** quite, **5.** too,
6. fairly, **7.** certainly, **8.** rather, **9.** much,
10. charming, **11.** suggests, **12.** uses, **13.** work,
14. decided, **15.** less

Page 36
1. gently, **2.** great, **3.** carefully, **4.** completely,
5. firmly, **6.** serious, **7.** fairly, **8.** entire, **9.** good,
10. well, **11.** well, **12.** good

Page 37
1. to her island, island; **2.** below the waves, waves;
3. without any means, means; of navigation,

navigation; except the stars, stars; **4.** For many centuries, centuries; by the stars, stars; **5.** in the 1700s, 1700s; **6.** on the sea, sea; of celestial navigation, navigation; **7.** of a star, star; **8.** above the horizon, horizon; **9.** from that reading, reading; **10.** Without this information, information

Page 38
1. in a car, in; **2.** from the sea, from; **3.** from the motion, from; of the waves, of; **4.** In this same way, In; in the back, in; of a car, of; **5.** of balance, of; **6.** inside your ears, inside; **7.** with a fluid, with; with special hairs, with; **8.** of movement, of; **9.** in the bottom, in; of the canals, of; **10.** around the canals, around; **11.** in your stomach, in; **12.–14.** Sentences will vary. Be sure that each sentence contains a prepositional phrase.

Page 39
1. preposition, **2.** adverb, **3.** preposition, **4.** adverb, **5.** preposition, **6.** adverb, **7.** preposition, **8.** preposition, **9.** preposition, **10.–13.** Sentences will vary. Be sure that each sentence contains a prepositional phrase.

Page 40
1. and, **2.** but, **3.** and, **4.** or, **5.** but, **6.** or, **7.** and, **8.** and, **9.** or, **10.** and, **11.** and, **12.** but

Page 41
1. Gee!, **2.** Wow!, **3.** Oh, dear!, **4.** Oh, my!, **5.** Good grief!, **6.** Oops!, **7.** Great!, **8.** Alas!, **9.** Of course! **10.–18.** Sentences will vary. Be sure that each sentence contains an interjection.

Unit 2

Page 42
1.–9. Sentences will vary. Be sure each sentence contains a subject or predicate as needed.

Page 43
1. We memorized the capitals of all of the states., **2.** Everyone knew the capital of Arkansas., **3.** The capital is not always the largest city in the state., **4.** You should picture the map in your mind., **5.** The left side is the west side., **6.** not a sentence, **7.** That river empties into the Gulf of Mexico., **8.** not a sentence, **9.** Three people found Delaware right away., **10.** not a sentence

Page 44
1. predicate, **2.** predicate, **3.** subject, **4.** subject, **5.** predicate; **6.** subject: The eye; predicate: is made of many parts., **7.** subject: The pupil; predicate: is the round, black center of the eye., **8.** subject: The outer, colored part; predicate: is called the iris., **9.** subject: The iris; predicate: is made of a ring of muscle., **10.** subject: Too much light; predicate: can damage the eye., **11.** subject: The iris; predicate: closes up in bright light., **12.** subject: Some people; predicate: are color-blind., **13.** subject: They; predicate: cannot see shades of red and green., **14.** subject: A nearsighted person; predicate: cannot see distant things well., **15.** subject: Close objects; predicate: are blurry to a farsighted person., **16.** subject: People who need glasses to read; predicate: are farsighted.

Page 45
1. Two young men, men; **2.** A raging tornado, tornado; **3.** Two square miles of the city, miles; **4.** An odd roaring noise, noise; **5.** The strong wind, wind; **6.** Giant walls, walls; **7.** One side of a street, side; **8.** The other side, side; **9.** Some people, people; **10.** A tornado, tornado; **11.** This lucky person, person; **12.** Unlucky people, people; **13.** Dorothy, Dorothy; **14.** She, She; **15.** A ride in a tornado, ride

Page 46
1. Sally and John; **2.** Roses, daisies, and violets; **3.** Jim and Meg, **4.** Sally, John, Jim, and Meg; **5.** A picnic basket and a jug of lemonade; **6.** The four friends and their two dogs; **7.** Apples, peaches, and plums; **8.** Frankie and Joanne, **9.** The six friends, the two dogs, and a few cats

Page 47
1. can be very interesting, can be; **2.** have found almost a million different types of insects, have found; **3.** live almost everywhere on Earth's surface, live; **4.** can study insects in the woods, streams, parks, and your own yard, can study; **5.** has no backbone, has; **6.** makes insects different from many animals, makes; **7.** have six legs, have; **8.** appeared about 400 million years ago, appeared; **9.** live together in large groups, live; **10.** capture insects and other small animals, capture; **11.** use the insects for food, use; **12.** attracts insects with its sweet nectar, attracts; **13.** snaps its leaves shut on insects, snaps; **14.** traps insects with a sticky liquid, traps

Page 48
1. planned and prepared; **2.** shopped, cleaned, and cooked; **3.** hired and bought; **4.** ordered and borrowed; **5.** wore and played; **6.** laughed and danced; **7.** cleared and helped; **8.** walked, ran, or rode; **9.** sat and rested

Page 49
1. subject: Our favorite coach, coach; predicate: cheers during the race, cheers; **2.** subject: My youngest sister, sister; predicate: swims ahead of the others, swims; **3.** subject: Her strokes, strokes; predicate: cut through the water, cut; **4.** subject: Ripples, Ripples; predicate: splash at the edge of the pool, splash; **5.** subject: The exciting race, race; predicate: ends with a surprise, ends; **6.** subject: My sister's team, team; predicate: finishes first, finishes; **7.** subject: The people in the bleachers, people; predicate: cheer wildly, cheer; **8.** subject: The team, team; predicate: holds the silver trophy for a school photograph, holds; **9.** subject: The team members, members; predicate: hug each other happily, hug; **10.** subject: Everyone in my family, Everyone; predicate: goes for an ice-cream cone, goes

Page 50
1. subject: house, it; predicate: was, had; compound; **2.** subject: Railroad; predicate: brought; simple; **3.** subject: wagons; predicate: were; simple; **4.** subject: rides; predicate: were; simple; **5.** subject: slaves, they; predicate: stopped, stayed; compound; **6.** subject: home; predicate: was; simple; **7.** subject: Levi Coffin, he; predicate: was, earned; compound; **8.** subject: Dies Drear, he; predicate: was, lived; compound; **9.** subject: Allan Pinkerton, he; predicate: made, hid; compound; **10.** subject: Harriet Tubman, she; predicate: led, took; compound

Page 51
Sentence types may vary.
1. ., declarative; **2.** ., declarative; **3.** ?, interrogative; **4.** !, exclamatory; **5.** ., imperative; **6.** ., declarative; **7.** ?, interrogative; **8.** !, exclamatory; **9.** ., declarative; **10.** ., imperative, **11.** ?, interrogative; **12.** ., imperative

Page 52
Students should circle sentences 2, 3, 4, 6, and 7.
1. Trash, **2.** (You), **3.** (You), **4.** (You), **5.** problem, **6.** (You), **7.** (You), **8.** Pieces, **9.–12.** Sentences may vary slightly. **9.** Avoid packages with too much wrapping., **10.** Buy the largest sizes of products., **11.** Use old T-shirts as wiping rags., **12.** Use both sides of writing paper.

Page 53
1. Chad and his friends, look; **2.** Chad, finds; **3.** He, pulls; **4.** rug, takes; **5.** friends, come; **6.** They, stand; **7.** Chad, explains; **8.** rug, tells; **9.** Chad and his friends, go; **10.** They, fly; **11.** Chad, wishes; **12.** he, hears; **13.** She, says; **14.** Chad; thanks, thinks

Page 54
Possible response: Each year, King Minos demanded a human sacrifice from the people of Athens. Seven boys and seven girls would enter the Labyrinth. The Labyrinth was the home of the Minotaur. The Minotaur was half man and half beast.

Page 55
1. Joanie waited patiently and quietly., adverbs; **2.** She had felt disappointed and rejected before., adjectives; **3.** She really and truly wanted to be a scientist., adverbs; **4.** Joanie read the letter slowly and calmly., adverbs

Page 56
1. Patrick studied the wall, and he found a hidden button., **2.** Patrick pushed the button, and the bookcase moved., **3.** Patrick could wait, or he could explore the path., **4.** He wasn't afraid, but he wasn't comfortable either.

Page 57
1. The sunlight shone on the little door., **2.** Into the shack walked Margaret and Danny., **3.** A large wooden table was inside the shack., **4.** A black cat lay on the table., **5.** Cannot be changed; inverting would change meaning., **6.** A witch's magic was at work in the shack!, **7.** Cannot be changed; inverting would change meaning.

Page 58
Corrections of sentences may vary. **1.** A box turtle is a reptile. It lives in woods and fields., **2.** Simple sentence, **3.** It can pull its legs, head, and tail inside its shell and get "boxed in.", **4.** Many kinds of turtles live on land and in the water., **5.** Turtles belong to the same family as lizards, snakes, alligators, and crocodiles., **6.** Simple sentence, **7.** Painted turtles eat meal worms, earthworms, minnows, and insects. The musk turtle finds food along the bottoms of ponds or streams., **8.** Painted turtles get their name from the red and yellow patterns on their shells. They also have yellow lines on their heads.

Page 59
Corrections of sentences may vary.
1a. You'll need 101 index cards. You'll need a colored marker.
1b. You'll need 101 index cards, and you'll need a colored marker.
2a. Print the name of a state or a state capital on each index card. Print the rules on the last index card.
2b. Print the name of a state or a state capital on each index card, and print the rules on the last index card.
3a. Put the marker away. Put all the cards in an envelope.
3b. Put the marker away, and put all the cards in an envelope.
4a. This game is for small groups. Up to three students may play.
4b. This game is for small groups, and up to three students may play.
5a. Players mix up the cards. They lay the cards face down.
5b. Players mix up the cards, and then they lay the cards face down.

Unit 3

Page 60
1. I was going camping with my friend Michael., **2.** We met Mr. Carl G. Carbur at the camping supply store., **3.** Michael and I decided that we needed a new tent., **4.** Mrs. Albright showed us many different tents., **5.** We chose one just like Dr. Pelky's., **6.** Michael's mother, Mrs. Mixx, gave us a ride to the campsite., **7.** After we set up the tent, I walked down the road., **8.** Dr. Pelky was at the next site!, **9.** Dr. Pelky was camping with Mario J. Moreno., **10.** Mario showed Michael and me a great place to fish., **11.** I caught some trout, and Michael caught a bass., **12.** Michael and I ate supper at Dr. Pelky's camp.

Page 61
1. My best friends and I plan to tour the United States., **2.** My friend Sandy is very excited because she has never been to California., **3.** She has never tasted any Mexican food, either., **4.** She will be coming from New York and meeting Jane in Philadelphia., **5.** Then, the two of them will pick up Roxanne in Phoenix, Arizona., **6.** When they get to San Francisco, I plan to take them out for Chinese food., **7.** If we go to Green's Restaurant for vegetarian food, even Jane will like the brussels sprouts., **8.** Sometimes I think that July will never get here., **9.** I received a letter from Sandy last Tuesday.

Page 62
1. I found a book of rhymes at the library in Milwaukee., **2.** The book was published in London, England., **3.** The book contained rhymes from the countries of Kenya, Ecuador, and even New Zealand., **4.** My favorite poem told of a crocodile that lived at the corner of Cricket Court and Bee Boulevard., **5.** We started driving across the Painted Desert Wednesday., **6.** Thursday morning we saw a beautiful sunrise., **7.** We decided to drive to the Rocky Mountains on Sunday., **8.** We finally reached El Paso, Texas, on Tuesday.

Page 63
Period placement: **1.** end of sentence, **2.** end of sentence, **3.** end of sentence, **4.** after Ms., end of sentence, **5.** after Dr., after B., **6.** after Dr., **7.** after T., R., end of sentence, **8.** after J., B., **9.** after N., after St., **10.** After I., A., B.

Page 64
1. My name is C. M. Dooley. I live at 4338 Market Blvd. in Alabaster, Alabama. My birthday is on Oct. 27., **2.** Suzy E. Ziegler requests the pleasure of your company at a party in honor of her friend, Maryanne M. Marbles. Please come to the country club at 23 Country Club Dr. at 4:00 on Tues., Apr. 14., **3.** The J. Harold Calabases take great pride in announcing the birth of their twins, Heather H. Calabas and J. Harold Calabas, Jr. This happy event took place on Mon., Aug. 23, at 3:00, **4.** F. A. Jones has been appointed assistant to the president of Bags and Boxes, Inc. This store is located at 45 Ninety-ninth Ave.

Page 65
1. Three plants to avoid are poison ivy, poison oak, and poison sumac., **2.** "Steven, I see that you have some poison oak growing in your yard.", **3.** "Your dog, cat, or rabbit can pick it up on its fur and rub against you," Wesley said., **4.** Yes, it will make your skin burn, itch, and swell., **5.** Dana put his clothes in a hamper, and his mother got a rash from touching the clothes., **6.** Poison ivy looks like a shrub, a vine, or a small plant., **7.** Poison ivy has green leaves in clusters of three, and so does poison oak.

Page 66
Comma placement: **1.** after interesting, **2.** after upstairs, **3.** after open, **4.** after room, **5.** after First, **6.** after Next, **7.** after while, **8.** after addition, **9.** after lived, after played, **10.** after footsteps, after whispers, **11.** after cellar, **12.** after Soon

Page 67
Comma placement: First letter: after Albuquerque, after April 22, after Dear Ernest, after Your friend,; Second letter: after Albuquerque, after May 3, after Dear David, after Sincerely

Page 68
1. ?, **2.** !, **3.** !, **4.** ?, **5.** ? , **6.** ?, **7.** !, **8.** !, **9.** !, **10.** ?, **11.** !, **12.** ?, **13.** !, **14.** ?, **15.** !, **16.** ?, **17.** !, **18.** !

Page 69
Apostrophe placement: **1.** Chen's, **2.** children's, **3.** boys', **4.** can't, **5.** Won't, Colon placement: **6.** 3:30, **7.** 6:00, **8.** 7:15, **9.** Dear Ms. Parker:

Page 70
1. You're, **2.** you'd, **3.** You'll, **4.** It's, **5.** won't, **6.** aren't, **7.** mustn't, **8.** don't, **9.** shouldn't, **10.** mustn't

Page 71
1. "Have you heard of the Nobel Peace Prize?" asked Emi., **2.** "Yes. Mother Teresa and Nelson Mandela have won it," replied Jan., **3.** "But do you know who Nobel was?" Emi asked., **4.** Jan responded, "No, I guess I don't.", **5.** "He invented dynamite," stated Emi., **6.** "It seems weird," said Jan, "to name a peace prize for the inventor of dynamite.", **7.** "In fact," Emi said, "dynamite was once called Nobel's Safety Blasting Powder.", **8.** "Nobel patented the blasting powder in 1867," Emi continued., **9.** "He did not want dynamite used for war," he said., **10.** He added, "Nobel once said that war is the horror of horrors and the greatest of all crimes.", **11.** "How did the Nobel Prizes get started?" asked Jan., **12.** Emi said, "In his will, Nobel said that his money should be used to establish prizes in five areas: physics, chemistry, medicine, literature, and peace.", **13.** "Sometimes a prize is shared by two or three people," he continued., **14.** "I'd like to know more about some of the winners," Jan said., **15.** "Jimmy Carter, the 39th president of the United States, won the Nobel Peace Prize in 2002," replied Emi.

Page 72
1. A Wrinkle in Time, **2.** "Camping in the Mountains", **3.** "It's Not Easy Being Green", **4.** Sounder, **5.** The New York Times, **6.** Humpty Dumpty, **7.** "The Little House", **8.** "Why I Like Gymnastics", **9.** The Little Prince, **10.** "The Owl and the Pussycat", **11.** The sixth chapter in that book is called "Animal Language", **12.** A book I really like is If I Were in Charge of the World by Judith Viorst.

Unit 4

Page 73
1. wisdom teeth, **2.** armchair, sunshine, **3.** ten-year-old, **4.** sky-high, birthplace, **5.** slave driver, bloodhounds, **6.** storm cellar, smokehouse, **7.** hand-to-mouth, run-ins, **8.** folksinger, notebook, **9.** run-of-the-mill, wallpaper, **10.** family tree, best-selling

Page 74
1. synonyms, **2.** antonyms, **3.** antonyms, **4.** synonyms, **5.** antonyms, **6.** synonyms, **7.** antonyms, **8.** antonyms, **9.** antonyms

Page 75
1. success, failure; **2.** left back, promoted; **3.** solution, problem; **4.** burning, ice-cold;

Answers in chart may vary. end: finish, begin; fast: quick, slow; simple: easy, complicated; gloomy: sad, upbeat; concealed: hidden, open; unsure: undecided, convinced

Page 76
Definitions may vary. **1.** unearthed, uncovered; **2.** nonexistent, does not exist; **3.** unable, incapable; **4.** discontinued, stopped; **5.** improbable, unlikely; **6.** inability, failure; **7.** resell, **8.** insincere, **9.** discomfort, **10.** mislead, **11.** prepay, **12.** unorganized or disorganized

Page 77
1.–12. Sentences will vary. New words: **1.** sailor, **2.** fearless or fearful, **3.** kindness, **4.** mighty, **5.** happiness, **6.** lighten, **7.** cloudy, **8.** suddenly, **9.** quietly, **10.** player, playful, **11.** wonderful, **12.** teacher

Page 78
1. air, **2.** you, **3.** course, **4.** would, **5.** need, **6.** main, **7.** mist, **8.** can, can; **9.** object, object; **10.** present, present; **11.** spring, spring

Page 79
1. week, **2.** way, **3.** find, **4.** know, **5.** do, **6.** through, **7.** see, **8.** beat, **9.** one; **10.–21.** Sentences will vary. Suggested homophones: **10.** pale, **11.** sun, **12.** flee, **13.** straight, **14.** too or to, **15.** meat, **16.** lead, **17.** side, **18.** blue, **19.** him, **20.** pain, **21.** horse

Page 80
1. to move in a boat; **2.** a ship, boat, or aircraft; **3.** something a person sets out to do; **4.** moved past or went by; **5.** gave a name to; **6.** arrived at or came to; **7.** ended or finished

Page 81
1. to, **2.** well, **3.** It's, **4.** your, **5.** Two, there, **6.** its, **7.** You're, **8.** too, **9.** good, **10.** They're, **11.** well, **12.** their, **13.** it's, **14.** two, **15.** They're

Page 82
1. will, **2.** a, **3.** are, **4.** anything, **5.** anybody, **6.** ever, **7.** any, **8.** There are no more than four kinds of poisonous snakes in North America., **9.** It won't do any good to try to run away from a rattlesnake.

Page 83
Sentences will vary. **1.** Our family was packing suitcases., **2.** Everyone was looking forward to our annual vacation., **3.** When all the suitcases were packed, Mom loaded the trunk., **4.** We left at noon on Saturday., **5.** We drove to the freeway., **6.** We stopped often because my little brother was ill., **7.** The first day of travel seemed fine, though., **8.** The second day we visited historical places., **9.** Everyone enjoyed the rest of the trip, too., **10.** Everyone welcomed us back.

Page 84
Senses may vary. **1.** blue, sight; **2.** cool, touch; **3.** large, sight; **4.** loud, hearing; **5.** chlorine, smell; **6.** jagged, touch or sight; **7.** rough, touch; **8.** soft, touch; **9.** warm, touch; **10.** delicious, taste

Page 85
1. wonderful, **2.** Brave, **3.** fascinating, **4.** hilarious, **5.** smile, **6.** cheap, **7.** soggy, **8.** nagged, **9.** stubborn, **10.** silly, **11.** A disaster is more serious than a problem., **12.** An antique is worth more than something old.

Page 86
Answers may vary. **1.** neutral, **2.** positive, **3.** neutral, **4.** negative, **5.** negative, **6.** negative, **7.** negative, **8.** positive, **9.** negative, **10.** positive, **11.–13.** Sentences will vary.

Page 87
Answers will vary. Possible responses are given. **1.** I was very nervous., **2.** As I looked out over the audience, my heart felt heavy., **3.** I touched the

piano keys, and my fingers were stiff., **4.** Luckily for me, the performance went very well., **5.** As I played the last notes, I knew that I had done well., **6.**–**7.** Responses will vary.

Page 88
1. as fast as the wind, **2.** They were able to whisper, "Hurry! Hurry!", **3.** It rode beside him like a good friend., **4.** They were enemies that caught at his sleeves., **5.**–**7.** Sentences will vary.

Unit 5

Page 89
Possible responses: Main Idea: how optical illusions occur; Detail: brain compares images you see to images in memory; Detail: brain cannot choose between possible interpretations; Detail: bending of light creates mirages that fool eyes

Page 90
1. b, **2.** a, **3.** b, **4.** a; Students should draw a line through these sentences: My mother went to India last year., Cinnamon and ginger come from India., The Ganges is a river in India.

Page 91
1. M, **2.** D, **3.** D, **4.** D; Paragraph: Main Idea: Many large factories have been built in southern Brazil., Detail: Some of these manufacturing plants produce cars, trucks, and farm equipment., Detail: Other products of these new factories include shoes, textiles, construction equipment, and leather products., Detail: Many of the goods produced in the factories of southern Brazil are shipped to the United States.

Page 92
1. He had a slow and serious nature., **2.** He was already an expert rider., **3.** The Crow Indians had stolen some Sioux horses., **4.** It was considered braver to push an enemy off a horse than to shoot an arrow from far away., **5.** Slow had jabbed the Crow with his stick., **6.** They had won the battle.

Page 94
1. Marc is sad because his friend Thomas is leaving., **2.** Marc finds a valuable coin that gives him an adventure and makes him happy., **3.** Marc and Mr. Ortiz have dialogue.

Page 96
Answers will vary.

Page 97
1. Thanksgiving, **2.** Thanksgiving has to be my favorite holiday., **3.** delicious aromas of turkey roasting and pumpkin pies baking; lovely autumn colors of orange, gold, red, and brown; sound of children laughing; music being played

Page 100
1. soft-drink machines in the park; **2.** The writer is against having soft-drink machines in the park.; **3.** Soft drinks have too much sugar in them, and they have no nutritional value. With soft-drink machines, the city has the problem of cleaning up the empty cans that are sometimes left in the park.; **4.** polite but firm

Page 103
1. pop popcorn in a microwave oven; **2.** Two items are listed, special microwave popcorn and a microwave oven.; **3.** Remove the plastic overwrap from the bag, and set it in the center of the microwave.; **4.** Set the microwave to full power.; **5.** Set the timer and start the oven.; **6.** Shake the bag before opening.

Page 106
1. Storing food in cans was developed in England in 1810.; **2.** Details may vary. Possible response: A British merchant named Peter Durchand came up with the idea. No one invented a can opener until 50 years later.; **3.** The can opener that we use today was invented about 1870.; **4.** Details may vary. Possible response: It was invented by an American named William W. Lyman. It has only been changed once since it was invented.

Page 109
1. The Tasady tribe and the Ik tribe are two examples of people still living in the Stone Age.; **2.** the Tasady and the Ik; **3.** Both are still primitive. Neither tribe knew about the outside world until recently. Both live in mountain areas.; **4.** The Tasady live in caves, but the Ik live in grass huts. The Tasady have plenty of food, but the Ik are always struggling to find food. The Tasady have a good chance of surviving, but the Ik do not.; **5.** contrast

Page 112
1. a girl named Katharine goes back in time; **2.** Merlin reversed Katharine's wish in the story.; **3.** Katharine would have won the jousting tournament instead of Sir Lancelot. Sir Lancelot would have been dismissed from the Queen's order of knights. King Arthur's Round Table would have been dissolved and never heard of again.

Page 114
Order of reasons will vary.

Page 115
1. how Mr. and Mrs. Hak-Tak made doubles of themselves; **2.** It was a very clever thing to do.; **3.** Keeping the doubles nearby was a clever way of protecting themselves.; **4.** Building a house next door for their doubles gave Mr. and Mrs. Hak-Tak extra help around the farm.; **5.** Their doubles became Mr. and Mrs. Hak-Tak's best friends.

Page 118
1. Wisconsin should have a "Caddie Woodlawn Day" to celebrate the trust between Caddie and her Indian friends.; **2.** "Caddie Woodlawn Day" would remind people to settle problems by peaceful means. Such a holiday would give people a reason to practice their ancestors' customs.; **3.** The state legislature should vote in favor of this idea.

Unit 6

Page 122
1. five, **2.** verb, **3.** noun, **4.** The balloon . . . 3, Have you . . . 5

Page 123
Sentences will vary. **1.** optical, **2.** reflection, **3.** magician, **4.** nature

Page 124
1.–**9.** Synonyms will vary. **10.**–**12.** Sentences will vary.

Page 125
1. Anthony, **2.** water, **3.** New, **4.** Scotland, **5.** Rio, **6.** United, **7.** literature, **8.** horses, **9.** Gila, **10.** Frost, **11.** Industrial, **12.** Victoria

Page 126
1. four, **2.** T 232, **3.** United States History, **4.** United States History, **5.** Origins, **6.** Black Americans

Page 127
Answers may vary. **1.** Sports, **2.** Reference Materials, **3.** Arts and Entertainment, **4.** Shopping, **5.** Games, **6.** Arts and Entertainment, **7.** Science or Reference Materials, **8.** Reference Materials

Page 128
1. Giants: In Myth and Legend, **2.** King Press, Inc., **3.** 1983, United States of America, **4.** 6, **5.** 2, **6.** 51, **7.** 73, **8.** 17

Page 129
1. two; hurricanes and tornadoes, **2.** causes of the storms, **3.** when and where the storms strike, **4.** tie it down securely, **5.** They could be broken by flying objects., **6.** when the authorities announce that it's safe

Page 130
Zeus's symbols were king's scepter, thunderbolt, oak tree, eagle.

Page 131
Notes will vary but should focus on main ideas and include abbreviations whenever possible. **1.** Responses will vary but should include a reference to key points or main ideas., **2.** Responses will vary but should include abbreviations for North America and California., **3.** Responses will vary but should include that good notes help the reader to remember key ideas.

Page 132
Answers may vary. Who: people from the northern United States; What: visit warmer places; Where: Florida's beaches; When: during the winter; Why: escape the cold; beaches and tourist attractions; Summary: Many Americans living in the north travel to Florida during the winter to escape the cold climate. They like to visit the beaches and many tourist attractions the state has to offer.

Page 133
1. Greg was angry because his mother had made him miss a movie with friends.; **2.** Greg was glad that he had not gone to the movies and gotten into trouble.

Page 134
1. c, **2.** e, **3.** a, **4.** d, **5.** b, **6.** f

Page 135
The Job of a Mother Bird; I. Find a Good Place for a Nest, A. correct, B. Warm enough, C. Out of reach of cats; II. Make the Nest, A. Big enough, B. correct, C. Sides tall enough, D. Inside soft enough; III. Take Care of Eggs, A. Sit on them, B. Keep them warm

Page 136
I. Cells, A. Smallest living parts of body, B. Building blocks, C. Many different kinds, 1. Bone cells, 2. Skin cells; II. Tissues, A. Groups of cells that work together, B. Many different kinds, 1. Fat tissue, 2. Muscle tissue, C. Each kind has a different function; III. Organs, A. Tissues that work together, B. Each has its own job, C. Need to work with other organs

Page 137
Topic and detail sentences will vary but should be related to the chosen outline.

Page 138
1. Elizabeth Dixon, **2.** Volume 18, **3.** Owl, November 1986, **4.** www.owltime.net, **5.** 24 March 2005

Page 139
Answers will vary. Possible responses are given. **1.** Our Old Superstitions, **2.** the superstition of knocking on wood, **3.** the superstition of opening umbrellas indoors, **4.** The custom is 4,000 years old. It began with some Native American tribes of North America. The oak tree was believed to be the home of the sky god.

Everything
I Need to
Know
I Learned at
Home

Everything I Need to Know I Learned at Home

An Encouraging Message for Moms

John Bytheway

DESERET
BOOK

Salt Lake City, Utah

Library of Congress Cataloging-in-Publication Data
CIP data on file
ISBN 978-1-60907-821-8

Printed in the United States of America
R. R. Donnelley, Crawfordsville, IN

10   9   8   7   6   5   4   3   2   1

To my mother:
Diane Jarman Bytheway

mother of six
grandmother of 36
great-grandmother of 19 and counting . . .

When my wife and I began raising our little family, people used to say, "Wow, you've got a house full of toddlers—what is it like being a dad?" My response was usually, "I look for shoes." For some reason, the thought of keeping their shoes on throughout the day was (and still is) completely foreign to my children. So they would take their shoes off, but they rarely remembered where they put them. Although it's not stated specifically in the proclamation on the family, my main job as a father, it seemed, was to look for shoes.

Of course, I would always ask my children to find their own shoes, but they would have the hardest time staying on task! "Sweetie, will you go get your shoes?"

I'd say, and my little girl would get about five feet away, and then she'd find something else to do. So I'd have to call her again. "Honey, I asked you to go get your shoes." She'd move maybe another five feet, and then she'd be distracted by something else. I discovered as a father that I had to repeat certain things over and over and over, without getting impatient, reminding myself that my daughter was just a little girl.

I also discovered that, because of the way we had our furniture arranged, the kids would often crawl themselves into a corner or get stuck behind a chair or sofa. After finding themselves in a mess of their own making, they'd look up at us and start crying with that "How could you let this happen to me?" expression on their faces. They couldn't even recognize that they were creating their own predicaments, but through it all, we just loved them more and more.

I've been fortunate because, for much of my life, I've been self-employed as a part-time teacher, part-time writer, and part-time shoe hunter, and have spent a lot of time at home. It's been a marvelous education for me to get a glimpse of what a home-maker does and to try to do it myself.

Growing up, I used to hear a set of basic phrases from my parents, and I find myself using them on my own children just as they did on me.

One common phrase was, "Wash your hands." My dad had an obsession with this. As dinnertime approached, we heard the familiar order, "Go wash your hands with hot, soapy water." One time, while heading for the bathroom sink, I joked with my sister, "No, we're going to use the cold, muddy water." Sometimes Dad would even check our water temperature, then inspect our hands! He would have rejoiced if he had lived to see the invention of hand sanitizer.

Another one we used to hear was, "Change your attitude." I heard that from my mom a lot (and from a number of my teachers, too). It was usually spoken after we had been asked to do something, a request that was followed by our predictable groaning, griping, and grumbling.

Another household phrase was, "Clean your

room." I suppose nearly everyone has heard that one. Actually, my mom had a rather odd way of putting it; she'd usually say, *"Pick up* your room," which I guess meant that I should pick up my toys and clothes that were *in* my room. As a kid, I always thought "Pick up your room" sounded funny. ("I can't pick up my room, Mom, it's too heavy.")

Another one I heard was, "Help your sister." We all heard that one from time to time because there were six of us, and the youngest of my siblings was a girl, and she often needed some help with this or that.

One of them was, "Go ask your dad," which usually came when we wanted to participate in some activity away from home that required the consent of both parents. I heard that one a lot, especially as I grew older.

And my very favorite one I used to hear was, "Come and eat." I've always liked that phrase. It carries its own sense of excitement, doesn't it? I still smile when I hear it—I just have to make a "hot, soapy water" stop on the way to the dinner table.

It dawned on me one day that all of these phrases that I heard so much as a child, these common household commands, are similar to the basic teachings of the gospel. In other words, *Everything I Need to Know I Learned at Home.* Think about it.

"Wash your hands." Spiritually speaking, to "wash your hands" means to repent, to be cleansed from sin, as in "Be ye clean that bear the vessels of the Lord" (D&C 133:5).

"Change your attitude." Our dispositions, our

A mother's heart is a child's schoolroom. The instructions received at the mother's knee . . . are never effaced entirely from the soul. . . . Family life is God's own method of training the young, and homes are largely what mothers make them. (Harold B. Lee, *Ye Are the Light of the World,* 295–96)

motives, and the intents of our hearts are important to the Lord. Each of us must be born again; we must have our hearts changed, healed, and renewed.

"Clean your room." In what kind of environment do we want to spend our lives? The scriptures answer this way: "Establish . . . a house of order" and "Stand ye in holy places" (D&C 88:119; 87:8).

"Help your sister." Service to others helps us to become what the Lord wants us to become. "By this shall all men know that ye are my disciples, if ye have love one to another" (John 13:35).

"Ask your dad." One of the most repeated commands in the scriptures is to pray to our Father in Heaven, and to pray often—even to pray "without ceasing" (1 Thessalonians 5:17).

And finally, **"Come and eat."** Isn't it wonderful that the Lord invites us to come and eat at the table of the Lord, to feast upon his love? Even in a gospel context, this phrase contains a sense of anticipation and enjoyment. Sweet is the work!

Let's spend a little more time looking at each of these phrases.

Wash Your Hands

In my childhood home, cleanliness was next to . . . impossible! There were just too many ways to get dirty as a kid. Spiritually speaking, staying perfectly clean is also impossible for mere mortals, since "all have sinned, and come short of the glory of God" (Romans 3:23). This creates quite a predicament, since "no unclean thing can dwell with God" (1 Nephi 10:21). We need someone to help us wash our hands.

Scriptures that describe returning to God's presence with unclean hands are absolutely terrifying. Alma the Younger taught, "The very thought of coming into the presence of my God did rack my soul with inexpressible horror" (Alma 36:14). Elsewhere he warned, "Our words will condemn us, yea, all our works will condemn us; we shall not be found spotless; and our thoughts will also condemn us; and in this awful state we shall not dare to look up to our God; . . . we would fain be glad if we could command the rocks and the mountains to fall upon us to hide us from his presence" (Alma 12:14).

Repentance is the "hot, soapy water" that can make us clean and prepare our souls so that instead of shrinking, or hoping that mountains will fall upon us and hide us, "[our] confidence [will] wax strong in the presence of God" (D&C 121:45).

Joseph F. Smith, while only a teenager, was serving a mission in Hawaii when in the midst of hardship and poverty, he had a remarkable dream:

> I dreamed that I was on a journey, and I was impressed that I ought to hurry—hurry with all my might, for fear I might be too late. I rushed on my way as fast as I possibly could, and I was only conscious of having just a little bundle, a handkerchief with a small bundle wrapped in it. I did not realize just what it was, when I was hurrying

as fast as I could; but finally I came to a wonderful mansion, if it could be called a mansion. It seemed too large, too great to have been made by hand, but I thought I knew that was my destination. As I passed towards it, as fast as I could, I saw a notice, "Bath." I turned aside quickly and went into the bath and washed myself clean. I opened up this little bundle that I had, and there was a pair of white, clean garments, a thing I had not seen for a long time, because the people I was with did not think very much of making things exceedingly clean. But my garments were clean, and I put them on. Then I rushed to what appeared to be a great opening, or door. I knocked and the door opened, and the man who stood there was the Prophet Joseph Smith. He looked at me a little reprovingly, and the first words he said:

"Joseph, you are late."

Yet I took confidence and said: "Yes, but

I am clean—I am clean!" (In Jack M. Lyon, Linda Ririe Gundry, and Jay A. Parry, eds., *Best-Loved Stories,* 248)

Repentance makes it possible for us to say, "I am clean, I am clean!"

Isaiah's testimony of the power of repentance is full of hope: "Though your sins be as scarlet, they shall be as white as snow; though they be red like crimson, they shall be as wool" (Isaiah 1:18).

Our spiritual hands may become soiled not only by sin but by earthly attitudes such as covetousness and materialism. Elder Jeffrey R. Holland observed, "Remember that in the end, surely God will be looking only for clean hands, not for full ones" ("To Y. Graduates: Books Not Closed," *Church News,* May 4, 1991).

Not only does the Atonement of Jesus Christ cleanse our hands, it changes our hearts. As we grow older and our experiences widen, our concern expands from having our hands clean to also having our hearts healed, which brings us to the second phrase I used to hear at home.

Change Your Attitude

There is a wonderful passage in the book of Psalms that describes multiple purposes of the Atonement: "Who shall ascend into the hill of the Lord? or who shall stand in his holy place?" (interestingly, the footnote on the words "holy place" refers to the temple). Verse 4 answers, "He that hath clean hands, *and* a pure heart" (Psalm 24:3–4; emphasis added). Perhaps *and* is the most important word in that verse. The Atonement of Jesus Christ does at least two things: It cleanses our hands *and* it purifies our hearts.

Elder Dallin H. Oaks taught this idea using a tree as an example. (I've always thought it was wonderfully appropriate that Elder *Oaks* would use a tree to illustrate a point.) He said:

A person who sins is like a tree that bends easily in the wind. On a windy and rainy day the tree may bend so deeply against the ground that the leaves become soiled with mud, like sin. If we only focus on cleaning the leaves, the weakness in the tree that allowed it to bend and soil its leaves may remain. Merely cleansing the leaves does not strengthen the tree. Similarly, a person who is merely sorry to be soiled by sin will sin again in the next high wind. The susceptibility to repetition will continue until the tree has been strengthened. . . . To be admitted to [God's] presence, we must be more than clean. We must also be changed from a weak person who has transgressed into a strong person with the spiritual stature to dwell in the presence of God. (*The Lord's Way*, 225–26).

It appears that King Benjamin's audience understood this dual purpose of the Atonement when they cried out, "Apply the atoning blood of Christ that we may receive forgiveness of our sins, *and* our hearts may be purified" (Mosiah 4:2; emphasis added). It is one thing to be cleansed from our sins, and quite another to have our hearts changed so that we no longer desire to sin. Thankfully, the Atonement of Christ does both.

Not only do our hearts need to be *changed,* but, very often, they need to be *healed.* Unrepented sin can make our hearts ache. But so can things that have hurt us in our past, or the injuries and aches brought on by the present poor choices of loved ones. I heard one woman say, "Most of my problems I either married or gave birth to." Actions of others can wound our hearts as severely, it seems, as our own actions do.

Jesus is a healer. Chapter 4 of the book of Luke recounts the return of Jesus after his baptism to his home in Nazareth. People had heard about him, and Luke reported that Jesus went to the synagogue, "as his custom was" (Luke 4:16), because he was about to announce his ministry. We can only imagine the tension and the drama as Jesus came back home. The custom was that a member of the congregation would get a scroll from the leader of the synagogue and stand up to read a passage; then he would sit down and make a comment about what he had just read. So Jesus stood up and received a scroll from the minister.

Now, here is the question: What passage should Jesus choose to read? He presumably had the entire Old Testament available to him, and he was about to choose a verse that would help him announce his divine identity and purpose. Suppose you had to pick a verse from the Old Testament that would best describe the Savior's mission—what verse would you pick? What verse would a religion professor choose? It's one thing to have Bible scholars pick a verse that they think might describe the Savior—we can probably all think of a few; "For unto us a child is born" (Isaiah 9:6) might be a good one, or "He was bruised for our iniquities . . . and with his stripes we are healed" (Isaiah 53:5). But it is quite another thing to have the Savior himself pick the verse, because his choice will tell us something about what *he* perceives his role to be. Is he going to choose a verse about punishment, or love, or sin, or judgment? Is he going to talk about how we all must repent and wash our hands? Jesus' choice is fascinating.

The Savior opened up the scroll to a passage his listeners would have recognized as coming from the prophet Isaiah. With all eyes upon him, Jesus read:

> The Spirit of the Lord is upon me, be-
> cause he hath anointed me to preach the
> gospel to the poor; he hath sent me to heal
> the brokenhearted, to preach deliverance to
> the captives, and recovering of sight to the
> blind, to set at liberty them that are bruised,
> to preach the acceptable year of the Lord.
> (Luke 4:18–19; compare Isaiah 61:1)

In my scriptures, I've underlined the words "poor," "brokenhearted," "captives," "blind," and "bruised." Which roles of the Messiah did Isaiah emphasize? He emphasized the Messiah's role as a *healer!* Yes, he will wash our hands; yes, he will be our judge; but what Jesus himself chose to emphasize was that he will heal our hearts, which is what we all long for.

But the story in Luke 4 isn't finished. Jesus returned the scrolls to the minister of the synagogue and sat down, and all in attendance waited to see what Jesus' commentary was going to be. And Jesus said (imagine this, it must have shaken the whole room), "This day is this scripture fulfilled in your ears" (Luke 4:21). What Jesus was saying was, "This is me—what I just read is referring to me." And this was dynamite because, notice the words, "The Spirit of the Lord is upon me, because he hath *anointed* me." *Messiah*, in Hebrew, means "anointed one." The word *Christ*, which is Greek, means "anointed one." In other words, Jesus arose and read, "The Spirit of the Lord is upon me, . . . he hath anointed me," then sat down and said, "That's me. I am the anointed one."

You may remember the argument that ensued: "Well, isn't this the son of Joseph?" And they thrust

Jesus out of the city, and tried to throw him off the brow of a hill, but he somehow passed through the crowd and escaped (see Luke 4:28–30). Bottom line, among all the roles Jesus has, he chose to emphasize his role as a healer of hearts; he came to heal the brokenhearted. How grateful we can be that the Atonement has those two major purposes: To cleanse our sins *and* to heal our hearts!

I've had the opportunity to speak in some difficult venues or difficult situations. One such speech was to the youth of the Columbine High School seminary shortly after the deadly school shooting there. Another was to the youth in Elizabeth Smart's stake two months after she was abducted, well before she was found. These assignments humbled me to the dust! At the latter event, the stake president got up and gave a better talk in about two sentences than I did in an hour. He said to the young people, "I want to talk to you about fear. The only thing we have to fear, ever, is sin." As I was sitting there in my chair, the more I thought about that, the more

I thought, "You know, we don't even have to fear that, because if we repent, then we don't even have to fear sin. The Savior can wash our hands and heal our broken hearts and he can restore that family in this life or the next." And what a wonderful miracle: the Smart family was restored and reunited in this life. Jesus Christ, the Messiah, purifies, changes, and heals hearts.

Clean Your Room

"Clean your room" was not a weekly phrase at my home, it was more like a daily phrase. We've often been counseled to maintain a spiritual environment in our homes, and, as we all know, this is getting harder and harder to do. I remember as a Boy Scout reading a pamphlet, the title of which I just can't remember. It must have been a Church publication, because I can't imagine a Boy Scout publication saying it exactly in this way, but I remember it encouraging me to keep a "righteous environment" so that the Spirit of the Lord would be comfortable in my room. I'd probably heard the same thing from my mom a hundred times, but for some reason those words in that setting made an impression on me, and I've wondered since if my mother secretly published that pamphlet. I couldn't let go of the idea, "Keep a righteous environment so the Spirit of the Lord can be in your room." It has always helped me keep the desire to keep my room clean because I felt the Lord

Women have always lifted entire cultures. Their influence begins in each society's very core—the home. Here women have taught and modeled what social historian Alexis de Tocqueville called "the habits of the heart," the civilizing "mores" or attitudes that create a sense of personal virtue and duty to the community, without which free societies can't exist. (Bruce C. Hafen, "Women and the Moral Center of Gravity," 291–92)

would be more likely to answer my prayers if my room was neat and orderly.

Today, our "spiritual environment" could include all of the various types of media we invite into our homes—everything from the Internet, YouTube, television, videos, and, of course, our music. When I teach the Book of Mormon, I always ask my students why the "great and spacious building" of Lehi's dream was described as being "in the air" (1 Nephi 8:26). I normally get this response, "Because it has no foundation." Which is a good answer, since a building without a foundation will eventually fall and crumble.

It is also strange to me that it is described as a "great and *spacious* building." The word *spacious* can only describe how big the building was on the inside, right? As in large, spacious rooms, or high ceilings. Isn't it odd, then, that in such a spacious building, the activity of choice was to go the windows and point? Elder Neal A. Maxwell once commented, "Considering their ceaseless preoccupation, one wonders, 'Is there no diversionary activity available to them, especially in such a large building—like a bowling alley?'" ("'Becometh As a Child,'" 68). And yet, the activity of choice was to ignore anything on the indoors and go mock those who were trying to partake of the love of God. And don't miss the footnote attached to the phrase "in the air." It refers the reader to Ephesians 2:2, where Paul refers to Satan as "the prince of the power of the air." Elder Bruce R. McConkie, commenting on Ephesians 2:2, stated that Satan's influence is "in, as it were, the very air around us" (*Doctrinal New Testament Commentary*, 2:499). Elder McConkie passed away in 1985, long before satellite TV and the Internet were household realities. Has there ever been a time when the influence of Satan was more "in the air" than it is now—I mean, literally? As you drive about your neighborhood, notice the satellite dishes on people's roofs, notice the wi-fi access available in fast-food restaurants, airports, and hotels, the wireless Internet for our computers and our iPhones and iPads—it's everywhere. It is a literal fulfillment of the phrase "in the air," making the counsel to keep our spiritual rooms clean more difficult than ever.

My mom often added another phrase after "clean your room," which was, "and take out the garbage." The media can, if we allow it to, deposit a considerable amount of garbage in our homes. The daily fare of television programs, what the chairman of the FCC once called a "vast wasteland," has now become more like a toxic waste dump. On a personal note, this is why I have every episode of *The Andy Griffith Show* at home on DVD. In 249 episodes (more than 100 hours of Emmy-Award–winning television), I cannot find one curse word. Ever. Not one instance of sex outside of marriage, or even the slightest vulgar innuendo. One hundred hours of television is, yes, a colossal waste of time, but in Mayberry, it's a clean waste of time.

Well, welcome to the twenty-first century. You are raising your children, and I am raising mine, in an environment where the days of *The Andy Griffith Show* and other programs like it are gone. Today, we'd be hard-pressed to find a sitcom in which there were no curse words, promiscuity, or vulgar innuendos. Indeed, the truths and values we embrace are mocked on every channel. That's how different things are today. And the Lord knows this.

President Boyd K. Packer spoke some comforting words about the challenge parents face in trying to keep their families clean within a darkening environment when he said, "The measure of our success as parents . . . will not rest solely on how our children turn out. That judgment would be just only if we could raise our families in a perfectly moral environment, and that now is not possible" ("Our Moral Environment," 68).

The mother and father of Ammon, Aaron, Omner, and Himni (the four sons of Mosiah) and the mother and father of Alma the Younger must have spent a lot of time on their knees on behalf of their sons. These boys went about not just knocking over mailboxes in the neighborhood. They were trying to *destroy the church of God!* How heartbreaking!

It's always been interesting to me that they got in trouble when they were with their friends. Often it seems that a teenager's IQ takes a nosedive when he or she is with friends. Can you imagine one of your teenagers saying, "I think I'll go to the mall and jump in the fountain by myself"? No way. But with their friends, you can almost hear them say, "Hey, that sounds like fun."

Parents love these verses in the book of Mosiah because they chronicle how help came in the form of an angel who knocked these five young men flat. Not only that, the angel explicitly stated that he came in response to a parent's pleading.

The Lord hath heard the prayers of his people, and also the prayers of his servant, Alma, who is thy father; for he has prayed with much faith concerning thee that thou mightest be brought to the knowledge of the truth; therefore, for this purpose have I come to convince thee of the power and authority of God, that the prayers of his servants might be answered according to their faith. (Mosiah 27:14)

"For this purpose have I come," the angel said. Perhaps we could pray for our own wayward children with this story in mind: "Heavenly Father, my children—excuse me, *your* children—are having some trouble. I'd like thee to knock them flat as the angel did with Alma the Younger and the four sons of Mosiah. And I'd like an angel with a thunderous voice, accompanied by a small earthquake—something between 6 and 7 on the Richter scale ought to do nicely. And feel free to knock them to the ground multiple times, as recorded in the Book of Mormon. Then have the angel chew them out until they've lost the strength in their limbs for a seventy-two-hour period. Then, if they could arise with the desire to serve a fourteen-year mission, that would be nice. And I say these things . . ."

Sometimes we wish we could do it that way, but

instead we have to trust the Lord and have the faith that he'll intervene in his way and in his time. We may not be able to secure the same type of angelic intervention that Alma the Younger experienced, but we do learn from this story that God hears the prayers of parents who are concerned about their children and their environment. We are also comforted to know that our children are his children too, and he loves them and "will order all things for [their] good" (D&C 111:11).

Brother S. Michael Wilcox gives a more modern example of the power of a parent's prayers. He had

> You can't possibly do this alone, but you *do* have help. The Master of Heaven and Earth is there to bless you. . . . Rely on Him. Rely on Him heavily. Rely on Him forever. (Jeffrey R. Holland, "'Because She Is a Mother,'" 36–37)

a student whose parents were undoubtedly praying about her. They were trying to help her develop her talents by providing music lessons, but she had taken those talents in a direction they hadn't intended and had joined a rock band. The changes in her personality and demeanor were clear to everyone but her. She had gradually and effectively rationalized away any discomfort about the clothing she wore to perform in, as well as the song lyrics and the questionable environments.

One night, when she went into her bedroom after a concert, she found herself looking at a poster on her wall that depicted the lead singer of a hard-rock band wearing chains. In her words:

"Suddenly, I felt as if the Savior entered my room, stood beside me, and looked at the poster with me. I think the Lord gave me a great gift, because I felt so ashamed. There was nothing desirable in the poster. I saw the whole rock industry for what it was. I tore down the poster, removed all other signs of rock from my room, and put up an old picture of the

Savior I'd had when I was a Mia Maid" (*Don't Leap with the Sheep,* 56).

Now, if we are going to trust the Lord, we must also trust his timing. We don't know when, we don't know how he'll intervene, but we know from Alma and from others that he will intervene. There will come a time. Some will learn only by the things that they experience, but they will learn, and they are his children.

Sometimes we quote Moses 1:39 to ourselves incorrectly; we imagine the Lord in a scolding posture saying to us, "For behold, this is *your* work and *your* glory—to bring to pass the immortality and eternal life of *your* children." Then we beat ourselves up with guilt when things aren't going well, or when we feel we are failing in our "work." But that's not what the Lord said! He said, "This is *my* work and *my* glory." And he is up to the task! In 2 Nephi 27:20, he said, "I am able to do mine own work." Our job description is to repent and to forgive, and his job description is to save. That's why we call him the Savior.

Elder Neal A. Maxwell observed:

> The Church's rising generation of young men and women are . . . *reserved* by the Lord for this time, [and] they must now be *preserved* by parents and *prepared* for their special moment in human history! They have been *held back* to come forth at this time, but now they need to be *pushed forward* to meet their rendezvous. . . .
>
> One final thought: just as the rising generation is here, now, by divine design—so are we who have been placed just ahead of them. Our lives and theirs have and will intersect many times before it is all over, and not by accident. ("'Unto the Rising Generation,'" 8, 11)

Help Your Sister

Years ago, I was invited to speak at a women's conference on the topic of competition. I thought it was a strange topic at first because the word *competition* made me think immediately of sports, and most of the women I know don't reach for the sports page when the newspaper comes. Then I thought of another, similar-sounding word: *comparing.* Sometimes, after comparing ourselves with others, we begin to see ourselves in competition with them as well, which can lead to a grab bag of other undesirable traits such as envy, resentment, and pride.

Even when we focus only on ourselves, we can get into trouble, since we measure ourselves in many different ways, some of which are good, and some of which are destructive. We may grade ourselves by our career, our waistline, our image, our home, our calling, our lifestyle, or a dozen other measurements.

Jesus, on the other hand, gave one key by which others could know where we stood in our relationship with him: "A new commandment I give unto you, That ye love one another; as I have loved you. . . . By *this* shall all men know that ye are my disciples, if ye have love one to another" (John 13:34–35; emphasis added). Notice the Savior didn't say, "This is how men will know: It will be by your car, it will be by your material success, or by your homemaking abilities." He didn't say, "This is how men will know: by your wardrobe, or by your physical fitness." Nope. He said, this is how they will know: By your "love one to another" (John 13:35). That's the measure Jesus gave for how we know that we are disciples. Instead of looking at others by comparing or competing, we are to look at one another as family.

Sister Patricia Holland told a story about her daughter, Mary, who was working on an entry for a talent contest sponsored by the PTA at her elementary school. Little Mary recorded in her journal:

> "I was practicing the piano one day, and it made me cry because it was so bad. Then I decided to practice ballet, and it made me cry more; it was bad, too. So then I decided to draw a picture because I knew I could do that good, but it was horrid. Of course it made me cry.

"Then my little three-year-old brother came up, and I said, 'Duffy, what *can* I be? What can *I* be? I can't be a piano player or an artist or a ballet girl. What can I be?' He came up to me and whispered, 'You can be my sister.'"

In an important moment, those five simple words changed the perspective and comforted the heart of a very anxious child. Life became better right on the spot, and as always, tomorrow was a brighter day. (Patricia T. Holland, "Filling the Measure of Your Creation")

Over the years, I've had the opportunity to attend the Hill Cumorah Pageant, the Nauvoo Pageant, and the Manti Pageant. Present at each of those events were groups of anti-Mormon protestors passing out leaflets and even lecturing us through megaphones about our errors. But I believe that Satan knows he's not going to destroy the Church from the outside in. His efforts, I believe, will be more focused on causing contention from the inside out. If he can get us gossiping about each other, being covetous and competing with each other, being rivals and opponents instead of brothers and sisters—that's how he is going to get us.

One of the most poignant moments I've ever seen while working with teenagers was at a huge "Best of Especially for Youth" conference in the Denver, Colorado, area. There were roughly 2,500 Latter-day Saint teenagers gathered at a convention center, and I was privileged to be one of the speakers. At the beginning of the program, one of the stake presidents stood at the podium and asked a particular young woman on the front row to stand up, turn around, and face her 2,500 peers—or, better said, her 2,500 brothers and sisters. The stake president called her by name and announced, "This young woman will be starting high school next month, and she will be the only Latter-day Saint in her entire school." And at that moment, as he had prearranged, all of the lights in this large room went dark except for a single spotlight on her. What happened next was one of the most encouraging things I've ever seen: The other 2,500 youth spontaneously stood up and started to cheer and applaud. I thought to myself, *She will never forget this.* And maybe when she

Can we love and support each other without judging each other harshly? So many of us are trying our hardest to live the commandments, often against great odds in our personal lives and unique family situations. Heaven knows, the world isn't giving us much support in these relationships. Let us support one another, even when—especially when—we differ on matters of personal choice and circumstance. Those are usually differences of preference, not principle. (Bruce C. Hafen, "Women and the Moral Center of Gravity," 300)

is at school and she's tempted or she's teased, she'll remember the moment when 2,500 of her brothers and sisters arose and said, "You can do this, and you are not alone. You go represent the Church to your school, and we'll go represent it to ours." If teenagers can do that for one another, then we adults can too.

I've thought since how wonderful it would be if we could gather all of the women of the Church together and do the same kind of thing: *This mom is raising her children all alone*—and we could all leap to our feet and give her our support. *This mom has to work to make ends meet*—and we could cheer and applaud her for doing what needs to be done. *This mom has many children and rarely gets a break*—and we could jump out of our seats and do the wave! *This sister adopted her children*—and we could show our admiration and support. *This woman has not married but she valiantly serves and moves forward*—and we could all rise to our feet and send the message, "We are with you, and you can be my sister" in the very best sense of that word.

I am reminded of something that I heard years ago: "Harmony is being different together." That's what we are called to do—to live in harmony. We can be different together. We can look at each other's talents and strengths and rejoice in the harmony of it all instead of engaging in the dissonance of comparing and competing. Comparing doesn't give us the results we want, so instead, we can celebrate our differences and be thrilled that somebody has a skill that we don't have.

When you feel overwhelmed or inadequate, when you feel worn out, when you feel underapprecieated

Fifty was my favorite age. It takes about that long to learn to quit competing—to be yourself and settle down to living. It is the age I would like to be through all eternity! (Marjorie Pay Hinckley, *Small and Simple Things*, 50.)

or overused or used up, just please remember your sisters around the world who would love to put their arms around you and say: "You are one of us, and you are our sister, and you can do this." And tomorrow, when you are underneath the table scraping up the spilled macaroni and cheese, or hunched over the sofa looking for the source of that awful smell, you can know that the wonderful women of the Church are with you.

You are a daughter of God. You are *not* a second-class citizen; it's the world that's second-class. You are not second-class because you are at home scraping macaroni and cheese out from under the table. A second-class world may try to make you believe that, but you won't hear it from your own family—and we are all siblings in the family of God.

Go Ask Your Dad

Please memorize this little verse: "Satan trembles, when he sees the weakest saint upon [her] knees" (William Cowper, in Oxford Dictionary, 161). Why would Satan tremble? Because he doesn't want you tapping into the power your Father in Heaven has. He doesn't want you to "ask your Father."

We had a painting in our home that I suppose many Latter-day Saints have, a picture of Jesus standing at the door and knocking. It is a depiction of Revelation 3:20, and to me, it's a perfect illustration of agency. When I was a child, my parents pointed out to me that the artist didn't paint a doorknob on the outside of the door "because this door," they explained, "can only be opened by you from the inside."

"Behold, I stand at the door, and knock: if any [woman] hear my voice, and open the door, I will come in" (Revelation 3:20). The Lord won't force himself into your heart and home. He respects your agency enough that he waits to be invited. The verse doesn't read, "Behold, I bust down the door and force you to accept my company."

Satan, on the other hand, has no such respect for agency. He comes uninvited and whispers things in our ears such as, "You are unworthy; you're a failure;

you can't pray; you don't deserve blessings," so that we *won't* go ask our Father. Nephi taught, "The evil spirit teacheth not a man to pray, but teacheth him that he must not pray. But behold, I say unto you that ye must pray always, and not faint; that ye must not perform any thing unto the Lord save in the first place ye shall pray unto the Father in the name of Christ" (2 Nephi 32:8–9).

President Gordon B. Hinckley recalled a story he heard from a woman in a panel discussion at the Tabernacle conducted by Elder Marion D. Hanks:

> Included in that panel was an attractive and able young woman, divorced, the mother of seven children then ranging in ages from five to sixteen. She said that one evening she went across the street to deliver something to a neighbor. Listen to her words as I recall them:
>
> "As I turned around to walk back home, I could see my house lighted up. I could hear

echoes of my children as I had walked out of the door a few minutes earlier: 'Mom, what are we going to have for dinner?' 'Can you take me to the library?' 'I have to get some poster paper tonight.' Tired and weary, I looked at that house and saw the light on in each of the rooms. I thought of all of those children who were home waiting for me to come and meet their needs. My burdens felt very heavy on my shoulders.

"I remember looking through tears toward the sky, and I said, 'Oh, my Father, I just can't do it tonight. I'm too tired. I can't face it. I can't go home and take care of all those children alone. Could I just come to You and stay with You for just one night? I'll come back in the morning.'

"I didn't really hear the words of reply, but I heard them in my mind. The answer was, 'No, little one, you can't come to me now. You would never wish to come back.

But I can come to you.'" ("What God Hath Joined Together," 71)

Note the promise within this verse in Isaiah: "Say to them that are of a fearful heart, Be strong, fear not: behold, your God will come . . . ; he will come and save you" (Isaiah 35:4). And I'd like to suggest that not only will he come to you, but he will run. And I'll back it up.

First, we're going to look at Alma 7:11–12. When we discuss this verse in my Book of Mormon classes, I ask my students to snap their fingers when they hear the word *sins*, since we know that Jesus died for our sins.

"And he [the Son of God] shall go forth, suffering *pains* and *afflictions* and temptations of every kind; and this that the word might be fulfilled which saith he will take upon him the *pains* and the *sicknesses* of his people. And he will take upon him *death,* that he may loose the bands of death which bind his people; . . . he will take upon him their *infirmities,* that his bowels may be filled with mercy, according to the flesh, that he may know according to the flesh how to succor his people according to their infirmities" (emphasis added).

I hope you noticed that Alma doesn't even mention sins in these two verses. As we discussed earlier, the Atonement not only cleanses our hands, it heals our hearts. But this verse also speaks of the eagerness of the Savior to help us. Let's take a look at the word *succor.*

When I was little, the word *succor* sounded like the item the drive-through bank teller handed my mom when she saw me in the backseat—a lollipop. In the 1828 *Webster's Dictionary,* succor is defined this way: "Literally, to run to, or run to support; hence, to help or relieve when in difficulty, want or distress; to assist and deliver from suffering" (in Dennis L. Largey, ed., *Book of Mormon Reference Companion,* 834). Inserting that definition into Alma 7:12, we get, "that he may know according to the flesh how *to run to* his people according to their infirmities." Not only will he come, he'll run.

Here's another place where this beautiful idea is taught. Luke 15 shares three parables of lost things—lost sheep, a lost coin, and lost sons. Let's take a look at the parable of the prodigal son:

> A certain man had two sons:
>
> And the younger of them said to his father, . . . give me the portion of goods that falleth to me. And he divided unto them his living.
>
> And not many days after the younger son gathered all together, and took his journey into a far country, and there wasted his substance with riotous living.
>
> And when he had spent all, there arose a mighty famine in that land; and he began to be in want.
>
> And he went and joined himself to a

citizen of that country; and he [the citizen] sent him [the son] into his fields to feed swine.

And he would fain have filled his belly with the husks that the swine did eat: and no man gave unto him.

And when he came to himself, he said, How many hired servants of my father's have bread enough and to spare, and I perish with hunger! "

In other words, My dad's servants are at my former home eating like kings, and I am out here feeding pigs, which, according to my law, I'm not even supposed to touch! And now I am the pigs' servant! Back home, my father's servants "have bread enough and to spare, and I perish with hunger!"

I will arise and go to my father, and will say unto him, Father, I have sinned against heaven, and before thee,

And am no more worthy to be called thy son: make me as one of thy hired servants.

And he arose, and came to his father. But when he was yet a great way off, his father saw him.

What does that tell you about where his father was? He was watching. He was looking, his face pressed against the window.

When he was yet a great way off, his father saw him, and had compassion, and *ran* (Luke 15:11–20; emphasis added).

If my son broke his mother's heart this way, I'm not sure I'd run to welcome him home. I might just wait on the porch and give the boy a tongue lashing. *So, you decided you had things pretty good here after all, eh?* But the father in the parable didn't talk, didn't wait, didn't scold. He ran, which in those times was not easy and not appropriate to do. Brother Robert L. Millet has explained: "In the Near East, for an elderly gentleman to run was disgraceful. He often had long, flowing robes, and running would require him to roll up his robes, allowing people to see his naked legs. That would be humiliating; it would be 'outlandish behavior'" (*Lost and Found,* 49–50).

But this father, overwhelmed by the love he felt for his son, ignored the conventions of the day and ran to him, "and had compassion, and ran, and fell on his neck, and kissed him" (Luke 15:20). We might wonder—was this boy's repentance complete? Probably not. It was just starting! And yet, the father ran and embraced him, and they walked back together.

As we know, the parable is not finished, and involves another son, but don't forget what we learn in this part—we've just learned that as soon as we turn to the Father, even when we're far away, he will run to us in whatever state we're in and help bring us home. Elder Bruce C. Hafen said: "Sometimes we say that no other success can compensate for our failures in the home. And while it is true that no other success *of ours* can fully compensate, there is a success that compensates for all our failures, after all we can do in good faith. That success is the Atonement of Jesus Christ. By its power, we may arise from the ashes of life filled with incomprehensible beauty and joy" (*The Broken Heart,* 22).

One of my favorite passages of scripture is in Doctrine and Covenants, section 19, written to Martin Harris, who used his wealth to help publish the Book of Mormon. Listen to what the Lord says to him about wealth, and how all the riches of the world pale in comparison to the opportunity of simple prayer and the universal blessing we all enjoy of being able to follow the counsel, "Ask your father."

> Pray always, and I will pour out my Spirit upon you, and great shall be your blessing—yea, even more than if you should obtain treasures of earth and corruptibleness to the extent thereof. Behold, canst thou read this without rejoicing and lifting up thy heart for gladness? (D&C 19:38–39)

What do you think will surprise you the most when you get to heaven? You can probably think of

a million things. I've enjoyed a little poem by an un-
known author that goes like this:

> *When you get to heaven*
> *You will likely view*
> *Many folks whose presence there*
> *Will be a shock to you,*
>
> *But keep it very quiet.*
> *Do not even stare.*
> *Likely there'll be many folks*
> *Surprised to see you there.*

Think of all the things that might surprise you
about heaven. Could it be the other people you meet?
And what does heaven look like? Are there trees? Are
there streets? Are there buildings? What does all that
look like? What will surprise you the most? The
answer may lie within my very favorite quotation
from President Ezra Taft Benson: "Nothing is going
to startle us more when we pass through the veil to
the other side than to realize how well we know our

Father and how familiar His face is to us" ("Jesus Christ—Gifts and Expectations," 6).

It's wonderful to know that the Father to whom we pray is so familiar! Brigham Young expressed the same idea a little more bluntly: "You know much about him, if you did but realize it. And there is no other one item that will so much astound you, when your eyes are opened in eternity, as to think that you were so stupid in the body" (in *Journal of Discourses,* 8:30).

President John Taylor added that our Father in Heaven is not the only one who is watching us: "God lives, and his eyes are over us, . . . his angels are round and about us, and they are more interested in us than we are in ourselves, ten thousand times, but we do not know it" (*Journal of Discourses,* 23:221).

Come and Eat

I love eating. And of all the things I've eaten, I think I enjoy food the most. Sometimes I marvel at the variety of fruits and vegetables and the textures and tastes that are available to us, and I think, "Wasn't it nice of the Lord to do that?" He must really love us, to provide us with such wonderful things, and do you know what? He tells us exactly that:

> Yea, all things which come of the earth, in the season thereof, are made for the benefit and the use of man, both to please the eye and to gladden the heart; yea, for food and for raiment, for taste and for smell, to strengthen the body and to enliven the soul. And it pleaseth God that he hath given all these things unto man; for unto this end were they made to be used, with judgment, not to excess, neither by extortion. (D&C 59:18–20)

The gospel is delicious food for the soul, and the Lord frequently invites us to "Come and eat." Lehi saw in vision that all mankind are invited to partake of the tree of life, which was "most sweet, above all that [he] ever before tasted" (1 Nephi 8:11). Nephi assures us we can dine for free: "Doth he cry unto any, saying: Depart from me? Behold, I say unto you, Nay; but he saith: Come unto me all ye ends of the earth, buy milk and honey, without money and without price" (2 Nephi 26:25). Nephi's brother Jacob invites us to enjoy a feast that lasts forever! "O all ye that are pure in heart, lift up your heads and receive the pleasing word of God, and feast upon his love; for ye may, if your minds are firm, forever" (Jacob 3:2).

Here's a good one you can stick on your fridge: "Come unto the Holy One of Israel, and feast upon that which perisheth not, neither can be corrupted, and let your soul delight in fatness" (2 Nephi 9:51).

Malachi referred to "the table of the Lord" (Malachi 1:7, 12), which we commonly think of as a table of communion with the Lord, or the sacrament table. Come and eat! Take the bread and the water each week. Alma alludes to Christ and to this symbolism when he says, "Come unto me and ye shall partake of the fruit of the tree of life; yea, ye shall eat and drink of the bread and the waters of life freely" (Alma 5:34).

Sadly, some refuse to come and eat, even when a banquet has been prepared and the food is ready. Jesus used the theme of a "great supper" for two of his parables (Matthew 22:1–14; Luke 14:16–24). In both of them, frustration and sadness are felt by the host when the invited guests refused to come. Imagine the disappointment! The Lord wants to serve us a meal of divine deliciousness—what could be better? Extensive plans have been made, a wonderful meal has been prepared, and no one wants to "come and eat"!

I hope my children know—not because I tell them, but because they can see it right in front of them—that the gospel is delicious to me, and that they too are invited to the feast.

Teaching the Gospel in Our Everyday Routines

When we first got married, I used to sleep through the night. I don't anymore. I think the kids conspire before they go to bed to keep me awake.

"Okay, I'll wake up at one a.m. screaming for no reason, then you fall out of bed at three, and I'll start making noise in the bathroom at five. We'll make sure Dad is up all night. Ready? Break!"

I get out of bed when I think I hear a noise. I walk around the house, making sure the doors are still locked. I peek out into the backyard to make sure no one has set up a campsite. Sometimes I walk down the hall and look at my kids in their bedrooms. And I suspect this has happened to you, so I

Mothers go longer on less sleep and give more to others with less personal renewal for themselves than any other group I know at any other time in life. It is not surprising when the shadows under their eyes sometimes vaguely resemble the state of Rhode Island. (Jeffrey R. Holland, "'Because She Is a Mother,'" 35)

---

am not saying anything new, but have you ever knelt down by your kid's bed in the middle of the night and just said: "Oh, Heavenly Father, please bless this one. Please bless my little girl that she'll be safe at school. There are so many dangers in this world, even people who are mean and abusive to children. Please protect this one." And I look at my little boy and say, "Please bless this one, Heavenly Father. Please protect all the children."

I am an imperfect father, and if I can feel that way about my children, don't you think our Father in Heaven often looks down at us in love? I wonder if sometimes he says, "Boy, my children, they just can't stay on task. I ask them to do something, and they can't get five feet before they're off track. They forget, so I tell them again and again and again; I repeat things over and over. And they get in messes and then look up at me and say, 'How could you let this happen to me?'" And yet Heavenly Father might say, "I love them more every day."

Every day, with all the little things you do in

your home, even in the little directions you give, in what may seem mundane, routine, and unexciting, you are actually teaching the gospel, and you can share these ideas with your children.

When you say, "Wash your hands," that may remind them, spiritually speaking, that each of us can repent and be clean.

When you say, "Change your attitude," you are reminding them on another level that the Savior can change our hearts, help us lose our desire to sin, and even heal our hearts when they are broken.

I hope you know that when you ask someone to clean their room, you are asking them to "stand in holy places," to purify their spiritual environment, or to make, in their own little space, "a house of order."

I hope you know that when you teach them about helping their brother or their sister, you are teaching your children to be disciples of Christ in our broader spiritual family. "By this shall men know" that we are his disciples—by our love one to another.

I hope that when you say, "It's okay with me, go ask your dad," that you will be reminded to close the day by asking your Father in Heaven in prayer to bless and watch over your family, so that he can come and run to you when you need strength.

And finally, I hope that when you say, "come and eat," you will find opportunities to teach your children that nothing is as satisfying as the gospel of Jesus Christ, who called himself the Bread of Life (see John 6:35) and promised that if we would eat of that Bread, we would never hunger again.

Sources

Benson, Ezra Taft. "Jesus Christ—Gifts and Expectations." *Ensign,* December 1988, 2–6.

Hafen, Bruce C. *The Broken Heart: Applying the Atonement to Life's Experiences.* Deseret Book, 1989.

———. "Women and the Moral Center of Gravity." In *Ye Shall Bear Record of Me: Talks from the 2001 BYU Women's Conference.* Deseret Book, 2002.

Hinckley, Gordon B. "What God Hath Joined Together." *Ensign,* May 1991, 71–74.

Hinckley, Marjorie Pay. *Small and Simple Things.* Deseret Book, 2003.

Holland, Jeffrey R. "'Because She Is a Mother.'" *Ensign,* May 1997, 35–37.

Holland, Patricia T. "Filling the Measure of Your Creation." BYU Devotional address, January 17, 1988. Available at speeches.byu.edu/?act=viewitem&id=378.

SOURCES

Journal of Discourses. 26 vols. Latter-day Saints' Book Depot, 1854–86.

Largey, Dennis L., general editor. *Book of Mormon Reference Companion.* Deseret Book, 2003.

Lee, Harold B. *Ye Are the Light of the World: Selected Sermons and Writings of Harold B. Lee.* Deseret Book, 1974.

Lyon, Jack M., Linda Ririe Gundry, and Jay A. Parry, eds. *Best-Loved Stories of the LDS People.* Deseret Book, 1997.

Maxwell, Neal A. "'Becometh as a Child.'" *Ensign,* May 1996, 68–70.

———. "'Unto the Rising Generation.'" *Ensign,* April 1985, 8–11.

The Oxford Dictionary of Quotations, 2nd ed. rev. 1966.

McConkie, Bruce R. *Doctrinal New Testament Commentary.* 3 vols. Bookcraft, 1965–73.

Millet, Robert L. *Lost and Found: Reflections on the Prodigal Son.* Deseret Book, 2001.

Oaks, Dallin H. *The Lord's Way.* Deseret Book, 1991.

Packer, Boyd K. "Our Moral Environment." *Ensign,* May 1992, 66–68.

Wilcox, S. Michael. *Don't Leap with the Sheep.* Deseret Book, 2001.